Abortion

Other Books in the Current Controversies Series

CURRENT CONTROVERSIES

Abortion

Tamara Thompson, Book Editor

GREENHAVEN PRESS
A part of Gale, Cengage Learning

GALE
CENGAGE Learning·

Farmington Hills, Mich • San Francisco • New York • Waterville, Maine
Meriden, Conn • Mason, Ohio • Chicago

Patricia Coryell, *Vice President & Publisher, New Products & GVRL*
Douglas Dentino, *Manager, New Products*
Judy Galens, *Acquisitions Editor*

For more information, contact:
Greenhaven Press
27500 Drake Rd.
Farmington Hills, MI 48331-3535
Or you can visit our Internet site at gale.cengage.com

For product information and technology assistance, contact us at

Gale Customer Support, 1-800-877-4253
For permission to use material from this text or product, submit all requests online at www.cengage.com/permissions

Further permissions questions can be emailed to permissionrequest@cengage.com

Articles in Greenhaven Press anthologies are often edited for length to meet page requirements. In addition, original titles of these works are changed to clearly present the main thesis and to explicitly indicate the author's opinion. Every effort is made to ensure that Greenhaven Press accurately reflects the original intent of the authors. Every effort has been made to trace the owners of copyrighted material.

Cover image © Anastasia Tveretinova/Shutterstock.com.

LIBRARY OF CONGRESS CATALOGING-IN-PUBLICATION DATA

Abortion / Tamara Thompson, book editor.
    pages cm. -- (Current controversies)
    Includes bibliographical references and index.
    ISBN 978-0-7377-7205-0 (hardcover) -- ISBN 978-0-7377-7206-7 (pbk.)
    1. Abortion--United States--Juvenile literature. I. Thompson, Tamara.
    HQ767.5.U5A222 2015
    362.1988'80973--dc23
                                                    2014030232

Printed in Mexico
2 3 4 5 6 7 19 18 17 16 15

Contents

Chapter 1: What Is the Current Landscape of the Abortion Debate?

Cheryl Wetzstein

Abortion has been legal in the United States for more than forty years, but the moral and political climate surrounding the issue is just as volatile today as it was when the Supreme Court handed down its landmark *Roe v. Wade* decision in 1973.

David Masci

Six in ten people surveyed by the Pew Research Center say they would not want to see abortion become illegal in the United States, a figure that has changed little over the past two decades.

M. Antonia Biggs, Heather Gould, and Diana Greene Foster

A recent study of the reasons women seek abortions found that the top three motivations are concerns about dramatic life changes, financial problems, and unstable relationships or the potential of being a single mother.

National Personhood Alliance

Based on the belief that human life begins at the moment of fertilization, the Personhood movement is pushing for legal recognition of fetuses as persons from the moment of conception forward. And while the group's focus is on abortion today, its longterm concern is with the evolving field of genetics.

Chapter 2: Can Abortion Be Morally Justified?

Even though polls show that Americans overwhelmingly support the right to abortion in cases of rape and incest, many anti-abortion groups support policies that deny government funding for such procedures or seek to ban them entirely.

No: Abortion Cannot Be Morally Justified

Chapter 3: Is Abortion Harmful to Women and Society?

Yes: Abortion Is Harmful to Women and Society

No: Abortion Is Not Harmful to Women and Society

A recent study in the United Kingdom found that although a woman experiencing an unwanted pregnancy is itself a risk factor for mental health problems, the risk is the same whether she terminates the pregnancy or gives birth.

Chapter 4: Should Access to Abortion Be Restricted?

Conscience laws allow health-care providers such as pharmacists and doctors to refuse to dispense medication or perform procedures, such as abortion, that conflict with their moral, ethical, personal, or religious beliefs. These laws are essential both to preserve the principle of individual freedom and to ensure the high quality of our health-care system.

No: Access to Abortion Should Not Be Restricted

Foreword

By definition, controversies are "discussions of questions in which opposing opinions clash" (*Webster's Twentieth Century Dictionary Unabridged*). Few would deny that controversies are a pervasive part of the human condition and exist on virtually every level of human enterprise. Controversies transpire between individuals and among groups, within nations and between nations. Controversies supply the grist necessary for progress by providing challenges and challengers to the status quo. They also create atmospheres where strife and warfare can flourish. A world without controversies would be a peaceful world; but it also would be, by and large, static and prosaic.

The Series' Purpose

The purpose of the Current Controversies series is to explore many of the social, political, and economic controversies dominating the national and international scenes today. Titles selected for inclusion in the series are highly focused and specific. For example, from the larger category of criminal justice, Current Controversies deals with specific topics such as police brutality, gun control, white collar crime, and others. The debates in Current Controversies also are presented in a useful, timeless fashion. Articles and book excerpts included in each title are selected if they contribute valuable, long-range ideas to the overall debate. And wherever possible, current information is enhanced with historical documents and other relevant materials. Thus, while individual titles are current in focus, every effort is made to ensure that they will not become quickly outdated. Books in the Current Controversies series will remain important resources for librarians, teachers, and students for many years.

In addition to keeping the titles focused and specific, great care is taken in the editorial format of each book in the series. Book introductions and chapter prefaces are offered to provide background material for readers. Chapters are organized around several key questions that are answered with diverse opinions representing all points on the political spectrum. Materials in each chapter include opinions in which authors clearly disagree as well as alternative opinions in which authors may agree on a broader issue but disagree on the possible solutions. In this way, the content of each volume in Current Controversies mirrors the mosaic of opinions encountered in society. Readers will quickly realize that there are many viable answers to these complex issues. By questioning each author's conclusions, students and casual readers can begin to develop the critical thinking skills so important to evaluating opinionated material.

Current Controversies is also ideal for controlled research. Each anthology in the series is composed of primary sources taken from a wide gamut of informational categories including periodicals, newspapers, books, US and foreign government documents, and the publications of private and public organizations. Readers will find factual support for reports, debates, and research papers covering all areas of important issues. In addition, an annotated table of contents, an index, a book and periodical bibliography, and a list of organizations to contact are included in each book to expedite further research.

Perhaps more than ever before in history, people are confronted with diverse and contradictory information. During the Persian Gulf War, for example, the public was not only treated to minute-to-minute coverage of the war, it was also inundated with critiques of the coverage and countless analyses of the factors motivating US involvement. Being able to sort through the plethora of opinions accompanying today's major issues, and to draw one's own conclusions, can be a complicated and frustrating struggle. It is the editors' hope that Current Controversies will help readers with this struggle.

Introduction

> "*Although* Roe v. Wade *is more than forty years old, the decision reverberates through American culture as strongly today as the day it was handed down.*"

Without question, the US Supreme Court's landmark *Roe v. Wade* decision legalizing a woman's right to abortion remains the country's most controversial, polarizing, and tempestuous issue more than forty years later. The ink was barely dry on the Court's 1973 ruling before states began enacting laws to severely restrict the practice, the first salvo in a long-running battle over whether to overturn *Roe* or protect the abortion access it guarantees. Four decades of legal challenges, court rulings, public protests, clinic blockades, violence, and ugly culture wars have done little to settle the matter, and the country remains hotly divided over the issue today.

As N.E.H. Hull and Peter Charles Hoffer write in the introduction to the second edition of their abortion movement history titled *Roe v. Wade: The Abortion Rights Controversy in American History*:

> *Roe*'s declaration that abortion was no longer a crime made the case into a symbol—for advocates of abortion rights a symbol of autonomy, of choice, and ultimately women's control of their reproductive lives; for women faced with the choice of an abortion, a source of soul-searching and often of guilt, for no one knows more immediately than the pregnant women that abortion ends a potential life; and for opponents of *Roe* a horror, not just for the violence it portended to a generation of "unborn," but for the disruption

of the home, the family, and the duties that women owed—or should have owed—to fathers, husbands, and children.[1]

To understand how a legal dispute over a medical procedure decided more than a generation ago became the cultural and political lightning rod that exists today it is essential to recognize the pervasive influence of *Roe*. Simply put, it is hard to find an aspect of American life that the case doesn't touch in some way.

First and foremost, *Roe* was a watershed moment in women's history; it upended long-entrenched social constructs of gender, sex, and class and fundamentally altered the balance of power between men and women. The reproductive rights guaranteed under *Roe* are closely tied to feminism and the social and economic empowerment of women, progress that is fiercely defended and celebrated by many.

The abortion debate is also closely tied to religious beliefs about conception and the sanctity of life, and many who oppose abortion do so as a faith-based matter of conscience, morality, or ethics. Following *Roe*, "conservative religion was a potent response to liberal feminism," write Hull and Hoffer, and that response forged a cultural schism. Abortion may have galvanized the women's rights movement, but it also galvanized religious objection. Consequently, "abortion became for some the symbol of women's liberation, and for others the harbinger of moral collapse."[2]

The legalization of abortion particularly inflamed Catholics and evangelical Christians, who coalesced to form the "pro-life" movement and argue that human life begins at conception and abortion is morally equivalent to murder. Over the years, that conviction gave rise not just to impassioned protests but to physically confrontational abortion clinic pick-

---

1. N.E.H. Hull and Peter Charles Hoffer, *Roe v. Wade: The Abortion Rights Controversy in American History*, 2nd ed., Lawrence: University Press of Kansas, 2010.

2. Ibid.

ets and barricades, vigilantism, and violence as some zealous activists killed abortion providers and firebombed clinics, particularly in the 1990s.

Aside from the very visible role doctors play on the front lines of the abortion conflict, *Roe* has influenced the medical profession in myriad ways. Most importantly, abortion goes to the very heart of the doctor-patient relationship, and *Roe* codified the privacy rights of that professional contract. Additionally, the desire to reduce the number of surgical abortions was the impetus for the US Food and Drug Administration's approval of medication abortion pills by prescription in 2000, as well as its nonprescription release of emergency contraceptives to all ages in 2013.

The two types of pills are now reshaping the reproductive-health landscape even further for a new generation of women. Twenty-three percent of all abortions are now done by medication, according to the Guttmacher Institute, a nonprofit research, education, and advocacy organization that deals with reproductive rights, and one in nine sexually active women had used emergency contraception as of 2010, a figure that is expected to grow significantly as more women become aware of its current status as a nonprescription drug.

Abortion plays a role in shaping broader health policies as well, by affecting public health outcomes and influencing US government funding of health care both domestically and around the world. More recently, abortion has played a central roll in opposition to the Affordable Care Act, President Barack Obama's signature health-care reform program.

Politically, abortion has been a flashpoint for partisanship ever since *Roe*, an inescapable litmus test for political candidates and judiciary appointees, especially Supreme Court nominees. Although not all Democrats are prochoice and not all Republicans oppose abortion, the partisan divide is quite clear and is reflected in the many ongoing legislative efforts surrounding the issue.

In the realm of law, abortion has figured prominently in the establishment of case law regarding privacy, governmental intrusion, due process, equal protection under the Fourteenth Amendment, protest, free speech, and youth rights in the United States. *Roe* arguably remains the most important building block of constitutional law since the country's founding—a "centerpiece of our constitutional history,"[3] as Hull and Hoffer describe it.

Although *Roe v. Wade* remains the law of the land in 2014, hundreds of laws explicitly crafted to restrict or discourage abortion have been enacted over the past forty-plus years. Some laws limit the specific procedures that can be performed, such as the 2003 federal ban on late-term, partial-birth abortion, while others generally define the circumstances under which a woman can obtain an abortion or under which a clinic or doctor can operate. State laws often include restrictions based on fetal age, a waiting period, mandatory viewing of information on fetal development or an ultrasound before the procedure, parental consent for minors, or consent of the fetus's father. Some jurisdictions even require doctors to provide information about supposed "risks" that are not medically substantiated, and others ban abortion almost entirely.

Most recently, after failing for so many years to get *Roe* overturned outright, the anti-abortion movement is focusing instead on putting so many burdensome restrictions on abortion that it becomes logistically impossible. So-called TRAP laws (for Targeted Regulation of Abortion Providers) at the state level institute licensing requirements that are deliberately difficult or impossible to satisfy, effectively shutting down clinics when they can't comply. More than half the states now have such laws on the books and numerous TRAP laws are being challenged in court by pro-choice groups.

3. Ibid.

The recent success the anti-abortion movement has had with TRAP laws was buoyed in part by the 2011 discovery of physician Kermit Gosnell's Philadelphia "house of horrors," in which the doctor performed hundreds of illegal late-term abortions under filthy conditions with "fetal remains haphazardly stored throughout the clinic—in bags, milk jugs, orange juice cartons, and even in cat-food containers," according to grand jury testimony in the case.

In May 2013, Gosnell was found guilty of murder for snipping the spinal cords of three infants who were born alive after twenty-four weeks of gestation. He was also convicted of twenty-one felony counts of illegal late-term abortion, one count of manslaughter for the death of an adult patient, and other serious charges. He was sentenced to life in prison without parole.

The Gosnell case horrified the American public and reignited a sense of purpose among anti-abortion activists, who have seen an uptick in public support for TRAP laws and a renewed willingness among members of Congress to consider anti-abortion bills, particularly those restricting late-term procedures.

"Using that case to justify regulating abortion clinics out of existence is a cynical ploy," states Rachel Benson Gold and Elizabeth Nash in an article in the *Guttmacher Policy Review*. "[T]hat is yet another obvious step in the march toward making safe abortion care even less accessible, if not illegal."[4]

While those who support abortion rights, such as Guttmacher, were equally repulsed by the Gosnell case, they maintain that restricting access to abortion and birth control is the

4. Rachel Benson Gold and Elizabeth Nash, "TRAP Laws Gain Political Traction While Abortion Clinics—and the Women They Serve—Pay the Price," *Guttmacher Policy Review*, vol. 16, no. 2, Spring 2013. http://www.guttmacher.org/pubs/gpr/16/2/gpr160207.html.

problem rather than the solution to preventing such atrocities. If women have easy access to birth control and safe and legal abortion, they argue, there would be no demand for butchers like Gosnell who jeopardize the lives of desperate women.

The two sides remain galaxies apart on the issue, underscoring the fact that although *Roe v. Wade* is more than forty years old, the decision reverberates through American culture as strongly today as the day it was handed down.

As Hull and Hoffer conclude, *Roe* deserves a place "in the long curve of history rather than [being isolated] as a self-contained moment. Although it is a landmark case in itself, its continuing influence on American law and politics prove that landmark cases live long beyond their formal resolution in courts of law."[5]

The authors in *Current Controversies: Abortion* examine the current landscape of the abortion debate and consider questions concerning whether abortion can be morally justified, whether it is harmful to women and society, and whether access to abortion should be restricted.

5. Op. cit.

CHAPTER 1

What Is the Current Landscape of the Abortion Debate?

Overview: Abortion Remains an Emotionally and Politically Charged Issue

Cheryl Wetzstein

Cheryl Wetzstein covers family and social issues as a national reporter for the Washington Times.

Forty years ago, a poor, anonymous, pregnant woman called "Jane Roe" stepped forward to attack a Texas state law banning abortion.

She and her attorneys succeeded beyond their wildest imaginations.

The U.S. Supreme Court's landmark *Roe v. Wade* ruling legalized a woman's right to abortion, overturned countless state laws and unleashed a cultural and political war so enduring that weeks after abortion supporters triumphantly swept pro-choice President [Barack] Obama into a second term of office, Catholic prelate Donald W. Wuerl felt compelled to publicly lament, "What is the spiritual climate in our country that allows this culture of death to prevail?"

More than 1 million abortions are performed each year in the United States, and an estimated total of 54 million pregnancies have been terminated since 1973, according to Guttmacher Institute data. But the moral and political questions surrounding the issue remain as unsettled in 2013 as they were 40 years ago [January 22, 1973], when the Supreme Court issued its 7-2 decision.

Abortion Wars

Abortion wars are under way in court and state legislatures over the "Obamacare" health care reform, and record numbers of abortion-regulating measures have been enacted at the state level in the past two years.

Abortion advocacy is also well-developed. In recognition of *Roe's* 40th anniversary, the pro-choice Advocates for Youth organization is championing the finding that about 30 percent of American women will have an abortion by age 45. It launched the "1 in 3" book and a campaign to tell women's stories about their abortions.

> *Although the abortion wars show no signs of easing, there are signs that the terrain on which the battles are being fought has shifted.*

In contrast, the Silent No More Awareness Campaign is continuing its efforts to help women talk about the regrets they feel over their abortions, while Feminists for Life tells young women that they "deserve better than abortion."

The annual March for Life protest, moved this year to Friday [January 25, 2013] because of Mr. Obama's inauguration ceremonies this week, remains one of the largest annual political protests staged on the streets of Washington, drawing marchers from across the country.

Although the abortion wars show no signs of easing, there are signs that the terrain on which the battles are being fought has shifted.

Prominent abortion rights advocacy groups have signaled that they will steer away from the "pro-choice" label.

"A growing number of Americans no longer identify with the 'pro-choice' and 'pro-life' labels that they believe box them in," said Cecile Richards, president of Planned Parenthood Federation of America. "Instead of putting people in one category or another, we should respect the decisions women and their families make," she said, releasing a video called "Not in Her Shoes," which urges Americans to start talking about abortion in a way "that doesn't divide you, but is based on mutual respect and empathy."

NARAL Pro-Choice America, with new President Ilyse Hogue, has introduced a "Choice Out Loud" campaign to expand the discussions.

"As a new generation of young people who support a woman's right to control her body and her life joins our ranks, the labels we use matter less," wrote Tarek Rizk, the group's communications director.

Pro-life leaders said they are not abandoning their brand.

"We will remain pro-life regardless of what the other side wants to call themselves," said Carol Tobias, president of the National Right to Life Committee.

Nobody is talking about dropping "life"—it's such a strong message, said Charmaine Yoest, president and chief executive of Americans United for Life. Moreover, she said, if people try to switch to talking about abortion rights and "women's health," "I say, 'Bring it on.' I would welcome a discussion about women's health."

The popular argument that abortion just removed a "blob of tissue" was undermined by technologies showing fetal development and "a beating heart" by the 22nd day of pregnancy.

Roe's Milestones

In the 40 years since the January 22, 1973, ruling in *Roe v. Wade*, many milestones have been reached.

In the 1970s and 1980s, the number of U.S. abortion clinics and legal abortions soared.

Abortion became a de facto "litmus test" for political candidates.

"A woman's right to choose" became a household phrase, and abortion rights supporters fiercely defended their views in courts and political arenas.

For years, a majority of Americans declared themselves pro-choice, according to the Gallup Poll.

Over time, pro-life forces found their voices, too.

The National Right to Life Committee and the annual March for Life were created after the Supreme Court ruling.

Pro-life members of Congress acted quickly to block taxpayer funding of abortion by passing the Hyde Amendment, named for the late Rep. Henry J. Hyde, Illinois Republican.

Developments on Both Sides

The popular argument that abortion just removed a "blob of tissue" was undermined by technologies showing fetal development and "a beating heart" by the 22nd day of pregnancy. Abortionist turned pro-lifer Dr. Bernard Nathanson's 1984 film, "Silent Scream," introduced the concepts of fetal awareness and distress during abortion.

Even "Jane Roe" switched sides: In 1995, Norma McCorvey announced that she had become a pro-life Christian.

The battles grew uglier in the 1990s as several abortion providers were fatally shot near their clinics or homes. As recently as 2009, abortion practitioner Dr. George Tiller was gunned down in his Kansas church.

Lawmakers reacted by creating "buffer zones" around clinics. Law enforcement officials brought justice to the killers, including clinic bomber Eric Rudolph, who evaded police for five years.

Since 2000, nonsurgical abortion methods, usually pills, were introduced to terminate early pregnancies.

These methods have given rise to "telemedicine" abortions, in which clinics use webcams to permit off-site doctors to counsel women and give them access to abortion pills. Because of telemedicine, the abortion industry is retaining doctors and serving rural clients.

Pro-life forces have responded by flooding most states with laws regulating abortions and clinics. Although some of these laws have been overturned or blocked in court, many states are curtailing abortions past 20 weeks because of a belief that fetuses can feel pain at that stage of gestation.

Shifting Views

Public attitudes also have shifted, and the pro-choice majorities of the past are steadily receding.

Last year, a record-low 41 percent of Americans identified themselves as pro-choice, according to the Gallup Poll, a significant drop from 1996, when 56 percent of Americans told Gallup they were pro-choice.

However, the national ambivalence about the choice between unlimited legal abortion and a blanket legal ban remains deep. Polls suggest that the true majority remains in support of legal abortion under certain circumstances: Last year, the plurality view (39 percent) was for "legal in only a few circumstances."

The rest of the Gallup respondents chose "legal under any circumstances" (25 percent), "illegal under all circumstances" (20 percent), "legal under most circumstances" (13 percent) or no opinion.

A recent Planned Parenthood poll of voters found that many people who say they are pro-life "also believe that women should have access to safe and legal abortion," Ms. Richards said, adding that this was part of the rationale to step away from the "choice" and "life" labels.

"It's a complicated topic and one in which labels don't reflect the complexity," she said.

But pro-life leaders said they will press forward and work closely with lawmakers in at least 39 states to enact more abortion laws, especially those to regulate clinics and "defund" abortion.

"Despite the fact that we saw a loss with the re-election of the most pro-abortion president we've ever seen, the pro-life movement right now is really, really gaining ground and developing momentum," said Ms. Yoest. "We are really energized right now."

Roe v. Wade at Forty: Most Oppose Overturning Abortion Decision

David Masci

David Masci is a senior research fellow for the Pew Forum on Religion & Public Life. He is also the Ira C. Lupu, F. Elwood, and Eleanor Davis Professor of Law Emeritus at George Washington University in Washington, DC.

As the 40th anniversary of the Supreme Court's *Roe v. Wade* decision approaches, the public remains opposed to completely overturning the historic ruling on abortion. More than six-in-ten (63%) say they would not like to see the court completely overturn the *Roe v. Wade* decision, which established a woman's constitutional right to abortion at least in the first three months of pregnancy. Only about three-in-ten (29%) would like to see the ruling overturned. These opinions are little changed from surveys conducted 10 and 20 years ago.

Decades after the Supreme Court rendered its decision, on Jan. 22, 1973, most Americans (62%) know that *Roe v. Wade* dealt with abortion rather than school desegregation or some other issue. But the rest either guess incorrectly (17%) or do not know what the case was about (20%). And there are substantial age differences in awareness: Among those ages 50 to 64, 74% know that *Roe v. Wade* dealt with abortion, the highest percentage of any age group. Among those younger than 30, just 44% know this.

The latest national survey by the Pew Research Center, conducted Jan. 9–13 [2013] among 1,502 adults, finds that abortion is viewed as a less important issue than in the past. Currently, 53% say abortion "is not that important compared to other issues," up from 48% in 2009 and 32% in 2006. The percentage viewing abortion as a "critical issue facing the country" fell from 28% in 2006 to 15% in 2009 and now stands at 18%.

However, the public continues to be divided over whether it is morally acceptable to have an abortion. Nearly half (47%) say it is morally wrong to have an abortion, while just 13% find this morally acceptable; 27% say this is not a moral issue and 9% volunteer that it depends on the situation. These opinions have changed little since 2006.

Wide Religious, Partisan Differences over *Roe*

There continue to be substantial religious and partisan differences over whether to overturn *Roe v. Wade*, and over the broader question of whether abortion should be legal or illegal in all or most cases.

There is no gender gap in opinions about Roe v. Wade: *Nearly identical percentages of women (64%) and men (63%) oppose reversing the decision.*

White evangelical Protestants are the only major religious group in which a majority (54%) favors completely overturning the *Roe v. Wade* decision. Large percentages of white mainline Protestants (76%), black Protestants (65%) and white Catholics (63%) say the ruling should not be overturned. Fully 82% of the religiously unaffiliated oppose overturning *Roe v. Wade*.

Half of Americans who attend religious services at least weekly favor completely overturning the *Roe v. Wade* decision, compared with just 17% of those who attend less often.

Republicans are evenly divided over whether the ruling should be overturned: 46% say it should, while 48% say it should not. By wide margins, Democrats (74% to 20%) and independents (64% to 28%) oppose overturning *Roe v. Wade*.

There is no gender gap in opinions about *Roe v. Wade*: Nearly identical percentages of women (64%) and men (63%) oppose reversing the decision.

Age and Awareness of *Roe v. Wade*

About six-in-ten Americans (62%) know that *Roe v. Wade* dealt with the issue of abortion. Much smaller percentages incorrectly associate the decision with school desegregation (7%), the death penalty (5%) or environmental protection (5%); 20% do not know.

Among those younger than 30, just 44% know that the case was about abortion; 16% say it dealt with school desegregation, and 41% either say it dealt with another issue (the death penalty or the environment), or do not know. Majorities of older age groups know that *Roe v. Wade* dealt with abortion.

There also are educational differences in awareness of which issue *Roe v. Wade* addressed. Fully 91% of those with post-graduate education know it dealt with abortion, as do 79% of college graduates, 63% of those with only some college experience and 47% of those with no more than a high school education.

Identical percentages of women and men (62% each) are aware that *Roe* dealt with abortion. Nearly seven-in-ten Republicans (68%) answered this question correctly, compared with 63% of independents and 57% of Democrats.

Views of Abortion's Importance

Slightly more than half of adults (53%) say that abortion is not that important compared with other issues. About a quarter (27%) say abortion is one among many important issues facing the country, while 18% view abortion as a critical issue.

Those who would like to see *Roe v. Wade* overturned are particularly inclined to view abortion as a critical issue facing the country. Nearly four-in-ten (38%) of those who support overturning the abortion ruling say abortion is a critical issue, compared with just 9% of those who oppose overturning *Roe v. Wade*. Among those who favor retaining *Roe*, 68% say abortion is not that important compared with other issues.

Nearly three-in-ten white evangelical Protestants (29%) view the issue of abortion as critical, compared with just 13% of white mainline Protestants and white Catholics. Majorities of white mainline Protestants (61%) and white Catholics (59%) say abortion is not that important compared with other issues. An even higher percentage of religiously unaffiliated Americans (71%) say abortion is relatively unimportant.

Abortion and Personal Morality

Nearly half of Americans (47%) say they personally believe that it is morally wrong to have an abortion, compared with 27% who say it is not a moral issue, 13% who find it morally acceptable and 9% who volunteer that it depends. These opinions have changed only modestly in recent years.

A majority of Republicans (63%) view having an abortion as morally wrong, compared with 45% of independents and 39% of Democrats.

There are deep differences among religious groups, as well as a wide partisan gap, in opinions about the moral acceptability of having an abortion.

Most white evangelical Protestants (73%), as well as 55% of white Catholics and 53% of black Protestants, say it is morally wrong to have an abortion. That compares with 36% of white mainline Protestants and just 20% of the religiously unaffiliated.

A majority of Republicans (63%) view having an abortion as morally wrong, compared with 45% of independents and 39% of Democrats.

Relatively small percentages of people in all religious, partisan and demographic groups say it is morally acceptable to have an abortion. However, nearly half of Democrats say either that having an abortion is morally acceptable (17%) or that it is not a moral issue (31%). Among independents, roughly four-in-ten say it is either morally acceptable (12%) or that abortion is not a moral issue (30%).

Those who favor overturning *Roe v. Wade* overwhelmingly say it is morally wrong to have an abortion; fully 85% express this view. Opinions about the morality of abortion are more divided among those who oppose overturning *Roe*. Nearly four-in-ten (38%) say abortion is not a moral issue, while 29% say having an abortion is morally wrong; just 17% of those who favor retaining *Roe* view abortion as morally acceptable.

Overall, nearly one-in-five Americans (18%) say they personally believe that abortion is morally unacceptable, yet also oppose the Supreme Court overturning its *Roe v. Wade* ruling.

Views of the Parties on Abortion

The survey finds that 41% say that the Democratic Party can do a better job of representing their views on abortion; nearly as many (36%) say the Republican Party could do better.

Last March, the Democratic Party held a 16-point advantage as better representing people's views on abortion (47% to 31%). In October 2011, the Democrats led by eight points on this issue (44% to 36%).

About the Survey

The analysis in this report is based on telephone interviews conducted January 9–13, 2013 among a national sample of 1,502 adults, 18 years of age or older, living in all 50 U.S. states and the District of Columbia (752 respondents were interviewed on a landline telephone, and 750 were interviewed on a cell phone, including 369 who had no landline telephone). The survey was conducted by interviewers at Princeton Data Source under the direction of Princeton Survey Research Associates International. A combination of landline and cell phone random digit dial samples were used; both samples were provided by Survey Sampling International. Interviews were conducted in English and Spanish. Respondents in the landline sample were selected by randomly asking for the youngest adult male or female who is now at home. Interviews in the cell sample were conducted with the person who answered the phone, if that person was an adult 18 years of age or older.

The combined landline and cell phone sample are weighted using an iterative technique that matches gender, age, education, race, Hispanic origin and nativity and region to parameters from the 2011 Census Bureau's American Community Survey and population density to parameters from the Decennial Census. The sample also is weighted to match current patterns of telephone status and relative usage of landline and cell phones (for those with both), based on extrapolations from the 2012 National Health Interview Survey. The weighting procedure also accounts for the fact that respondents with both landline and cell phones have a greater probability of being included in the combined sample and adjusts for household size among respondents with a landline phone. Sampling errors and statistical tests of significance take into account the effect of weighting. . . .

In addition to sampling error, one should bear in mind that question wording and practical difficulties in conducting surveys can introduce error or bias into the findings of opinion polls.

Women Seek Abortions for a Variety of Complex Reasons

M. Antonia Biggs, Heather Gould, and Diana Greene Foster

M. Antonia Biggs is a senior researcher at Advancing New Standards in Reproductive Health (ANSIRH), a collaborative research group and think tank at the University of California, San Francisco (UCSF)'s Bixby Center for Global Reproductive Health. Heather Gould is the research coordinator for the Turnaway Study, and Diana Greene Foster is interim director of ANSIRH.

While the topic of abortion has long been the subject of fierce public and policy debate in the United States, an understanding of why women seek abortion has been largely missing from the discussion. In an effort to maintain privacy, adhere to perceived social norms, and shield themselves from stigma, the majority of American women who have had abortions—approximately 1.21 million women per year—do not publicly disclose their abortion experiences or engage in policy discussions as a represented group.

A review of several international and a handful of US qualitative and quantitative articles considered reasons for abortion among women in 26 "high-income" countries. Of these, four studies (two primarily quantitative, one primarily qualitative and one that used mixed methods) were conducted in the US. This review found that, despite methodological differences among the studies, a consistent picture of women's reasons for abortion emerged, that could be encapsulated in three categories:

1. "Women-focused" reasons, such as those related to timing, the woman's physical or mental health, or completed family size;

M. Antonia Biggs, Heather Gould, and Diana Greene Foster, "Understanding Why Women Seek Abortions in the US," *BMC Women's Health*, 2013. Copyright © 2013 by BMC Women's Health. Licensed under CC by 2.0.

2. "Other-focused" reasons, such as those related to the intimate partner, the potential child, existing children, or the influences of other people; and

3. "Material" reasons, such as financial and housing limitations.

These categories were not mutually exclusive; women in nearly all of the studies reported multiple reasons for their abortion.

The largest of the US studies included in the review, by [L.B.] Finer and colleagues, utilized data from a structured survey conducted in 2004 with 1,209 abortion patients across the US, as well as open-ended, in-depth interviews conducted with 38 patients from four facilities, nearly half of whom were in their second trimester of pregnancy. Quantitative data from this study were compared to survey data collected from nationally representative samples in 1987 and 2000. The most commonly reported reasons for abortion in 2004 (selected from a researcher-generated list of possible reasons with write-in options for other reasons) were largely similar to those found in the 1987 study.

While the US abortion rate appears to have stabilized after a national decline, this decline has been slower among low-income women and in certain states.

The Top Three Reasons

The top three reason categories cited in both studies were:

1. "Having a baby would dramatically change my life" (i.e., interfere with education, employment and ability to take care of existing children and other dependents) (74% in 2004 and 78% in 1987),

2. "I can't afford a baby now" (e.g., unmarried, student, can't afford childcare or basic needs) (73% in 2004 and 69% in 1987), and

3. "I don't want to be a single mother or am having relationship problems" (48% in 2004 and 52% in 1987).

A sizeable proportion of women in 2004 and 1987 also reported having completed their childbearing (38% and 28%), not being ready for a/another child (32% and 36%), and not wanting people to know they had sex or became pregnant (25% and 33%).

Considering all of the reasons women reported, the authors observed that the reasons described by the majority of women (74%) signaled a sense of emotional and financial responsibility to individuals other than themselves, including existing or future children, and were multi-dimensional. Greater weeks of gestation were found to be related with citing concerns about fetal health as reasons for abortion. The authors did not examine associations between weeks of gestation with some of the other more frequently mentioned reasons for abortion.

While the US abortion rate appears to have stabilized after a national decline, this decline has been slower among low-income women and in certain states, suggesting possible disparities in access to effective contraceptive methods and/or economic challenges preventing women from feeling they are able to care for a child. According to national estimates for 2005 and 2008, changes in the abortion rate varied by region, with the South and West seeing small declines, and the Northwest and Midwest seeing no change over that period.

Furthermore, the changing political climate and increasing restrictive legislation with regards to abortion in this country, in conjunction with the economic recession, may be affecting women's reasons for seeking abortion, warranting a fresh investigation into these issues. This study builds upon and extends the small body of literature that documents US women's reasons for abortion.

While two other papers using data from the Turnaway Study (see below) describe how women who indicate partner related reasons or reasons related to their own alcohol, tobacco and/or drug use, differ from those who do not mention these reasons this study presents all of the reasons women from the Turnaway Study gave for seeking abortion, as described in their own words.

Study Methods

This study was approved by the University of California, San Francisco, Committee on Human Research. Written and oral consent was obtained from all participants.

Data for this study were drawn from baseline quantitative and qualitative data from the Turnaway Study, an ongoing, five-year, longitudinal study evaluating the health and socioeconomic consequences of receiving or being denied an abortion in the US. . . .

A financial reason (40%) was the most frequently mentioned theme [for getting an abortion]. Six percent of women mentioned this as their only reason for seeking abortion.

All participants were asked two open-ended questions about their reasons for seeking an abortion. The first question asked "What are the reasons that you decided to have an abortion?" followed by a prompt asking for any other reasons until the respondent says that is all. The second questions asked "What would you say was the *main reason* you decided to have an abortion?" Generally participants were not able to narrow their answers to one reason and sometimes even gave additional reasons to this last question making it difficult to discern a "main" reason. Therefore, the answers to both questions were combined to identify all reasons given by respondents for seeking abortion. . . .

Women gave a wide range of responses to explain why they had chosen abortion. The reasons were comprised of 35 themes which were categorized under a final set of 11 overarching themes. While most women gave reasons that fell under one (36%) or two (29%) themes, 13% mentioned four or more themes. Many women reported multiple reasons for seeking an abortion crossing over several themes. As one 21 year-old woman describes, "This is how I described it [my reasons for abortion] to my doctor 'social, economic', I had a whole list, I don't feel like I could raise a child right now and give the child what it deserves." A 19-year old explains, "[There are] so many of them [reasons]. I already have one baby, money wise, my relationship with the father of my first baby, relationship with my mom, school." A 27-year old enumerates the reasons that brought her to the decision to have an abortion, "My relationship is newer and we wanted to wait. I don't have a job, I have some debt. I want to finish school and I honestly am not in the physical shape that I would want to be to start out a pregnancy."

Financial Reasons

A financial reason (40%) was the most frequently mentioned theme. Six percent of women mentioned this as their only reason for seeking abortion. Most women (38%) cited general financial concerns which included responses such as "financial problems," "don't have the means," "It all boils down to money" and "can't afford to support a child." As one unemployed 42-year-old woman with a monthly household income of a little over $1,000 describes, "[It was] all financial, me not having a job, living off death benefits, dealing with my 14 year old son. I didn't have money to buy a baby spoon."

A small proportion of women (4%) stated that lack of employment or underemployment was a reason for seeking an abortion. A 28-year old college educated woman, receiving $1,750 a month in government assistance, looking for work, and living alone with her two children while her husband was away in the Air Force explains "[My husband and I] haven't had jobs in awhile and I don't want to go back to living with other people. If we had another child it would be undue burden on our financial situation." Six (0.6%) women stated that their lack of insurance and/or inability to get government assistance contributed to their desire to terminate their pregnancies.

> I'm unemployed, no health insurance, and could not qualify for any government-assisted aid, and even if my fiance decided to hurry up and get married, I still wouldn't have been covered under his health insurance for that. 32-year-old, in school full-time.

Nearly one third (31%) of respondents gave partner-related reasons for seeking an abortion.

Four respondents (0.4%) said that their desire to have an abortion stemmed from their inability to provide for the child without relying on government assistance. "I don't have enough money to support a child and I don't want to have to get support from the government."

Not the Right Time for a Baby

Over one third (36%) of respondents stated reasons related to timing. Many women (34%) used phrasing such as "I wasn't ready" and "wasn't the right time." A 21-year old pointed to a number of reasons why she felt the timing of her pregnancy was wrong "Mainly I didn't feel like I was ready yet—didn't feel financially, emotionally ready. Due date was at the same time as my externship at school. Entering the workforce with a newborn would be difficult—I just wasn't ready yet." A small proportion of women described not having enough time or feeling too busy to have a baby (2%). A 25-year old looking for work, already raising a child, and who reported "rarely" having enough money to meet her basic living needs explains how she has, "So many things going on now—physically, emotionally, financially, pretty busy and can't handle anymore right now." Similarly, a 19-year old describes how she "didn't have time to go to the doctor to make sure everything is OK like I wanted to. So busy with school and work I felt it [having an abortion] would be the right thing to do until I really have time to have one [a child]." Few women described being too old to have a baby (2%). A 43-year old illustrates how timing and her age are the primary reasons for seeking abortion "Because I'm too old to have a child. It's like starting over and my nerves are bad. My son, he's going to be 20 next month and I don't want to start over. It's just bad timing."

Partners and Other Children

Nearly one third (31%) of respondents gave partner-related reasons for seeking an abortion. Six percent mentioned partners as their only reason for seeking abortion. Partner related reasons included not having a "good" or stable relationship with the father of the baby (9%), wanting to be married first (8%), not having a supportive partner (8%), being with the "wrong guy" (6%), having a partner who does not want the baby (3%), and having an abusive partner (3%). . . .

The need to focus on other children was a common theme, mentioned by 29% of women. Six percent of women mentioned only this theme. The majority of these reasons (67%) were related to feeling overextended with current children, "I already had 2 kids and it would be really overwhelming. It's kind of hard to raise 2 kids by yourself," that the pregnancy was too soon after a previous child. "I have a 3-month-old already. If I had had that baby, he wouldn't even be one [year old by the time the baby came]", or simply not wanting any more children, "I just felt inadequate—I have a teenager and 2 pre-teens and I couldn't see starting over again." A small proportion (5%) of women felt that having a baby at this time would have an adverse impact on her other children. "I already have 5 kids; their quality of life would go down if I had another." A 31-year-old with three children spoke of the need to focus on her sick child as a reason for seeking abortion. "My son was diagnosed with cancer. His treatment requires driving 10 hours and now we found out we need to go to New York for some of his treatment. The stress of that and that he relies on me."

Nineteen percent of respondents (19%) described feeling emotionally or mentally unprepared to raise a child at this time.

A New Baby Would Interfere with Future Opportunities

One in five women (20%) reported that they chose abortion because they felt a baby at this time would interfere with their future goals and opportunities in general (5%) or, more specifically, with school (14%) or career plans (7%). Usually the reasons were related to the perceived difficulty of continuing to advance educational or career goals while raising a baby: "I didn't think I'd be able to support a baby and go to college and have a job," states an 18-year old respondent in high school. A 21-year-old woman in college with no children explains that she "Still want[s] to be able to do things like have a good job, finish school, and be stable." Similarly, a 26-year old desiring to go back to college explains "I wanted to finish school. I'd been waiting a while to get into the bachelor's program and I finally got it." Another woman explains "I feel like I need to put myself first and get through college and support myself." As a 21-one-year old seeking a college degree points out, "I'm trying to graduate from college and I'm going to cooking school in August and I have a lot of things going for me and I can't take care of a kid by myself." Others spoke to the inability to take time off work to raise the child. A 21-one-year old holding two part-time jobs and raising two children states: "I wouldn't be able to take the time off work. My work doesn't offer maternity leave and I have to work [to afford to live] here. If I took time off I would lose my job so there's just no way."

Some women, particularly younger women, expressed the feeling that having a baby at this time would negatively impact multiple aspects of their future lives.

> It is hard to get in school. If I had the baby it would be tough to do school work, thinking about my future. I know that I wouldn't be able to do what I want to do. I still want to be free and have my youth. I don't want to have it all gone because of one experience. I still want to study abroad. I don't want to ruin that. —20-year-old in college with no children

Approximately 5% of respondents explained that their living or housing context was not suitable for a baby and mentioned this as one of the reasons they chose abortion.

Not Emotionally or Mentally Prepared

Nineteen percent of respondents (19%) described feeling emotionally or mentally unprepared to raise a child at this time. Respondents in this category were characterized by a feeling of exasperation and an inability to continue the pregnancy—"I can't go through it," "I just felt inadequate"—or feeling a lack of mental strength to have the baby—"[I am] not mentally stable to take that on, emotionally, I couldn't take care of another baby," and "I couldn't handle it." A 19-year old mother reporting a history of depression and physical abuse describes seeking an abortion because, "I have a lot of problems— serious problems and so I'm not prepared for another baby." Another woman explained her rationale for seeking abortion, "I would say a mental reason, in the sense that it would really be a burden because then I would have to watch three, my hands are already full."

Health-Related Reasons

Twelve percent of respondents (12%) mentioned health-related reasons ranging from concern for her own health (6%), health of the fetus (5%), drug, tobacco, or alcohol use (5%), and/or non-illicit prescription drug or birth control use (1%). Maternal health concerns included physical health issues that would be exacerbated by the pregnancy or due to the pregnancy itself, "My bad back and diabetes, I don't think the baby would have been healthy. I don't think I would have been able to carry it to term" as well as mental health concerns. Five percent of women (5%) chose abortion because they were concerned about the effects of their drug and/or alcohol use on the health of the fetus or on their ability to raise the child. . . . Other women (5%) voiced concern for the health of the fetus because they had been using contraceptives (n=4), psychotropic drugs (n=3) or medications (such as antibiotics, blood thinners, and narcotics) to treat other health conditions (n=7). As one woman explains, she and her partner chose abortion "because I had been doing drinking and the medication I'm on for bipolar disorder is known to cause birth defects and we decided it's akin to child abuse if you know you're bringing your child into the world with a higher risk for things."

Want a Better Life for the Baby than She Could Provide

Twelve percent of women gave reasons for choosing abortion related to their desire to give the child a better life than she could provide. Responses related to generally wanting to give the child a better life (7%) were characterized by a concern for the child, "I'm afraid my kid will be suffering in this world" and "wouldn't have been good for me or the child," or a feeling of inadequacy to parent the child: "I can't take care of a kid because I can barely take care of myself and I don't want to bring a child into the world when I'm unmarried and not ready." As reflected in this previous quote, sometimes statements stemmed from a desire for the baby to have a father, or the feeling that the father of the baby was not suitable. "I didn't want to do it by myself. I couldn't and the man was abusive and horrible. I didn't want my kid to grow up with a father like that (knowing his father had left)." For one woman, the decision to terminate her pregnancy was a moral one. "I've been unemployed it's not a decision I can face morally without being able to raise it properly. An abortion was the best option."

Approximately 5% of respondents explained that their living or housing context was not suitable for a baby and mentioned this as one of the reasons they chose abortion. According to a 22-year old who described herself as being unable to work, on welfare, and rarely having enough money to meet basic living needs: "My mom pays my rent for me and where I live I can't have kids. I can't get anyone to rent to me because I have had an eviction and haven't had a steady job."

While never mentioned as the only reason for choosing abortion, 13 respondents said that lack of help to care for the baby was one reason they chose abortion. Responses included "I wouldn't have a babysitter for school," "family isn't close by to help", and "My grandma passed away and she was the one who was going to help." Another subcategory of this theme included choosing abortion because of the desire not to repeat their childhood (n=5). An 18-year old who frequently smoked marijuana explained that she chose abortion, "Because I did do drugs and my mom used drugs with me and my sister and

I swore to myself I wouldn't bring a child into this world like that." Another respondent in her teens and who had a history of physical and sexual abuse and neglect remarked "my childhood was less than awesome, if I do have a child I want to give it the best possible life that I can and I am not in a place to do that right now."

Four percent (4%) of women gave reasons falling under the theme not wanting a baby or not wanting to place a baby for adoption.

Personal and Family Reasons

Less than 7% of women explained that their reliance on others or lack of maturity was a reason for choosing abortion. Some women felt they were too young (5%), unable to take care of themselves (1%), or too reliant on others to raise this baby (1%). "I'm not grown up enough to take care of another person. I can't take care of myself yet, let alone another person. I wouldn't want to bring a baby into this world with parents who aren't ready to be parents."

Around 5% of women described a concern for, or influences from family or friends as a reason for seeking abortion. Two percent feared that having a baby would negatively impact their family or friends, "It would have been a strain on my family" and a similar proportion (2%) didn't want others to know about their pregnancy or feared judgment or reaction from others. A 19-year old explains that the reason she chose abortion was because "I was scared to go to my parents." Another woman feared what the family would think about her having a biracial child. A small minority reported influences or pressure from family or friends (n=11) as a reason for seeking abortion. "Because my mother convinced me to get one," explains one 17-year old. A 23-year old describes her rationale for seeking abortion "because my dad thinks I should finish school first, not financially ready for a baby, gonna have to move out when I have the baby." Similarly, a 25-year old explained that she wanted an abortion because of, "the negative feedback I was getting from my family."

Four percent (4%) of women gave reasons falling under the theme not wanting a baby or not wanting to place a baby for adoption. Three percent (3%) explained succinctly that they do not want a baby or don't want children. "I just didn't want any kids. It [a baby] is something I just didn't want." A small number (n=7) mentioned adoption was not an option for them. As one 25-year old describes, "We are not really sure if we ever want kids. I don't think that I would be strong enough to give it up for adoption." Another respondent states that, "adoption isn't an option for me—so it was kind of a no brainer decision."

Eleven women (1%) gave other reasons for seeking abortion that didn't easily fall into one of the major themes, including going through legal issues (n=3) and fear of giving birth (n=2).

Women who chose abortion because they felt having a baby would interfere with her future plans were more likely to be younger, to have more than a high school education, self-rated good health, and lower scores on the pregnancy intentions scale.

Factors Related to Reasons for Abortion

Using mixed effects multivariate logistic regression analyses, we examined the social and demographic predictors of the predominant themes women gave for seeking an abortion. Significant predictors of reporting financial reasons for seeking an abortion included marital status, education level, and not having enough money to meet basic living needs. Women who gave financial reasons for seeking an abortion were more likely to have a higher level of education, less likely to be separated, divorced or widowed than to be single/never married, and less likely to have enough money to meet basic needs. Approximately 82% of women who reported this as a reason were single/never married.

Women who reported reasons related to the need to focus on other children now were significantly more likely to have a lower pregnancy intentions score, and, to have a greater number of children. All women who reported this as a reason had one or more children.

Women who reported that this is not the right time for a baby as a reason for seeking abortion had a lower pregnancy intentions score and lower parity. Over half (51%) of women who reported this as a reason had no children.

Women who gave partner related reasons were significantly more likely to be African American, and to have higher parity. Older women, women who were separated, divorced or widowed, and women with higher pregnancy intention scores, had increased odds of giving partner related reasons.

Women who chose abortion because they felt having a baby would interfere with her future plans were more likely to be younger, to have more than a high school education, self-rated good health, and lower scores on the pregnancy intentions scale. Among those who reported this as a reason, over half (52%) were in college or getting their Associates or technical degree.

A Variety of Predictors

Predictors of reporting being emotionally or mentally unprepared as a reason for seeking abortion included race/ethnicity and having enough money to meet basic living needs. Women who were African American were less likely than white women to report this as a reason. Women who reported having sufficient money to meet basic needs were at a reduced odds of reporting this as a reason for seeking abortion.

Women with a history of depression or anxiety had sharply elevated odds of mentioning physical or mental health factors as reasons for seeking abortion. Women who rated their health as good and were employed had reduced odds of mentioning physical or mental health reasons for seeking abortion.

Women who chose abortion because they wanted to give the baby a better life than they could provide were significantly more likely to have more than a high school education, have lower parity, and to lack a usual health care provider. Over half of women who gave this as a reason were nulliparous (55%).

Women who gave lack of independence or immaturity as a reason for seeking abortion were more likely to be younger and lower parity. All women who gave this reason were under age 31, 48% were in their teens and 83% were nulliparous. Marital status was excluded in the model because of problems with collinearity with the outcome. Nearly all (97%) women who gave this as a reason were single/never married.

Reporting influences from friends and family as a reason for seeking abortion was significantly predicted by age and pregnancy intentions. Women who report this reason were more likely to be younger and to have a higher pregnancy intentions score. Over three quarters (85%) of women who gave this as a reason were ages 24 and under. Their average pregnancy intentions score was higher when compared to women giving other reasons.

The two significant predictors of "don't want a baby or place baby for adoption" were lower parity, and a lower pregnancy intentions score. Over two thirds (68%) who reported this reason were nulliparous.

Discussion of Results

The findings from this study demonstrate that the reasons women seek abortion are complex and interrelated. Unlike other studies, this study asked women entirely open-ended questions regarding the reasons they sought to terminate their pregnancies, ensuring that all women's reasons could be fully captured. This methodology enabled us to get a wide range of responses that otherwise would not have been gathered. While some women stated only one factor that contributed to their desire to terminate their pregnancies, others pointed to a myriad of factors that, cumulatively, resulted in their seeking an abortion.

Among women without fetal anomalies, reasons for seeking abortion are not different whether women sought abortion early or late in pregnancy.

As indicated by the differences we observed among women's reasons by individual characteristics, women seek abortion due to their unique circumstances, including their socioeconomic status, age, health, parity and marital status. Even with changes in the climate surrounding abortion and the shifting demographics of the women having abortions, the predominant reasons women gave for seeking abortion reflected those of previous studies. Reasons related to timing, partners, and concerns for the ability to support the child and other dependents financially and emotionally were the most common reasons women gave for seeking an abortion, suggesting that abortion is often a decision driven by women's concerns for current and future children, family, as well as existing commitments and responsibilities. Some women held the belief that her unborn child deserves to be raised under better circumstances than she can provide at this time; in an environment where the child is financially secure and part of a stable and loving family. This intersection between abortion and motherhood is described qualitatively in a study by [R.K.] Jones and colleagues where women indicate that their abortion decisions are influenced by the idea that children deserve "ideal conditions of motherhood." Some women also seem to have internalized gendered norms that value women as self-denying and always thinking in the best interest of her children, over making self-interested decisions. Experiences of stigma, fear of experiencing stigma, or internalized stigma around her abortion may have prompted women to give more socially desirable responses to make her appear or feel selfless, to justify her abortion decision. Other studies have reported abortion-seeking women's fear of being judged as having made a selfish decision. At the same time, some of the women seeking abortion in this study were aiming to secure themselves a better life and future—chances for a better job and a good education. These women may be more stigmatized than the former since they don't fall into a discourse of the selfless and all-sacrificing woman. In an effort not to further contribute to the abortion stigma in our culture, we must be careful not to use women's reasons for abortion as a way to rationalize or justify their abortions, but rather to better understand their experiences.

Denying women an abortion, which occurred among one quarter of the women interviewed in this study, may have a significant negative impact on her health, her existing children and other family members, and her future. Policies that restrict access to abortion must acknowledge that such women will need added support (e.g. financial, emotional, educational, health care, vocational support) to appropriately care for their children, other children, and themselves. In some cases, where women are struggling with abuse or health issues, continuing an unwanted pregnancy to term may be associated with even greater than normal risks of childbirth.

Study Limitations

This study should be viewed in light of its limitations. Fewer than 40% of women who were eligible and approached agreed to participate. Many women may have been deterred from enrolling because participation required bi-annual interviews for a period of 5 years. Nonetheless, our sample demographics,

with the exception of our over-representation of women beyond the first trimester, closely mirror the national estimates
of women seeking abortion in the US, suggesting that our results are generalizable. The greater proportion of women in
our sample seeking abortions at later gestational ages and
without fetal anomalies allows us to make inferences about a
previously understudied group. Gestational age at the time of
the interview was unrelated to any of the major themes mentioned. Other studies have found that late gestational age was
an important predictor of termination because of concerns
about the health of the fetus. In this study, we have excluded
women seeking abortion for fetal anomaly and found that
seeking a later abortion was unrelated to women's reasons for
seeking an abortion. Thus, among women without fetal
anomalies, reasons for seeking abortion are not different
whether women sought abortion early or late in pregnancy.
This suggests that factors other than the reasons for desiring
an abortion play a role in seeking later abortions.

---

*It is important that policy makers consider women's mo-
tivations for choosing abortion.*

A small number of women stated that concern for the fetus while using contraception or other medications was a reason for seeking abortion pointing to an area for intervention.
The general consensus in the literature is that birth control
use during pregnancy is unlikely to have negative consequences
for the development of the fetus. A better understanding of
the potential impact of the contraceptive methods and other
medications on a developing fetus can help women be better
informed when deciding whether nor not to have an abortion.

Outside Influence and Pressure

Laws requiring waiting periods, mandated counseling, and parental involvement for adolescents are motivated in part by a
desire to protect women from making uninformed decisions

and from being coerced into having an abortion. Prior research suggests that, women who feel the abortion decision is not completely their own have more difficulty coping following an abortion. Our study, like most studies of women seeking abortions, finds that few women report pressure from others as a reason for seeking abortion. About 1% of women in this study described being influenced by others to have an abortion. Our study design, however, did not allow us to assess the level of pressure women experienced. The pressure women felt may have varied in degree from statements of a mild lack of support for continuing a pregnancy to strong and specific statements about a lack of future emotional or financial support for the pregnancy or potential child. While these women's pregnancy intention scores are somewhat higher than those who gave other reasons for abortion, their scores were still in the unintended/ambivalent range. Health care providers should continue to assess and confirm that women are able to make their own decision about whether or not to continue or end a pregnancy. Women who experience pressure may benefit from additional emotional support if they choose to proceed with abortion.

In recent years, politicians, advocacy organizations and the media have extensively debated issues related to the funding, provision, utilization, and morality of abortion, and legislation restricting abortion access has increased dramatically. The Guttmacher Institute documented that 92 new provisions restricting abortion were enacted in 2011, almost three times the previous record of 34 provisions enacted six years earlier.

Policy Implications

Despite the proliferation of proposed legislation that would restrict access to abortion, the public discourse concerning why women seek abortions has been limited. It is important that policy makers consider women's motivations for choosing abortion, as decisions to support or oppose such legislation could have profound effects on the health, socioeconomic outcomes and life trajectories of women facing unwanted pregnancies.

As found in previous literature, the findings from this study demonstrate that women are motivated to seek abortion for a wide range of reasons that are driven by their unique circumstances and stage of life. Women expressed lacking the financial, emotional, and physical resources to adequately provide for a/another child, yet many were denied access to a wanted abortion. Supporters of policies that continue to further restrict women's access to abortion need to recognize the potential impact on the financial, emotional, and physical well-being of these women and their families. Women who carry an unwanted pregnancy to term because they are denied access to a wanted abortion may require financial assistance, support handling an abusive partner, access to mental health services prenatal care and, potentially, specialized health care for high risk pregnancies. By better understanding women's decisions when faced with an unintended pregnancy and de-stigmatizing abortion seeking we can better support women's reproductive decisions and provide them with the resources they may need.

The Modern Personhood Movement—What Is It?

National Personhood Alliance

The National Personhood Alliance (NPA) is a Bible-based confederation of organizations and pro-life leaders who believe that the strategy of pursuing personhood is essential in order to end abortion.

Personhood is a shift back to a Christ-centered view on the sanctity of life and all dignity of life issues. We begin with a recognition of the dignity of the human person at all stages of development due to the image of God in all human beings, the *imago Dei*.

To understand the Personhood strategy, you simply have to look at three passages in the Bible, which are easy to remember, Genesis 1, Jeremiah 1 and Luke 1.

> *Genesis 1:26* "Then God said, 'Let Us make man in Our image, according to Our likeness.'"

> *Jeremiah 1:5* "Before I formed you in the womb I knew you; Before you were born I sanctified you; I ordained you a prophet to the nations."

> *Luke 1:39–45* "Now Mary arose in those days and went into the hill country with haste, to a city of Judah, and entered the house of Zacharias and greeted Elizabeth. And it happened, when Elizabeth heard the greeting of Mary, that the babe leaped in her womb; and Elizabeth was filled with the Holy Spirit. Then she spoke out with a loud voice and said, 'Blessed *are* you among women, and blessed *is* the fruit of

your womb! But why *is* this *granted* to me, that the mother of my Lord should come to me? For indeed, as soon as the voice of your greeting sounded in my ears, the babe leaped in my womb for joy. Blessed *is* she who believed, for there will be a fulfillment of those things which were told her from the Lord.'"

A Pro-Life Paradigm Shift

Personhood represents a paradigm shift in the pro-life movement in that we begin with scripture and insist that the right to life is God-given in that we are all created in the image of God and were made in God's image from our biological beginning in the womb.

Years ago, I first heard someone say that the political end of the pro-life movement failed at its inception because it was never Christ-centered and you can't fight a demonic force with natural weapons. We hear the phrase, "You can't fight Goliath in Saul's armor." This means that man's efforts will fail, but God's plan for victory is according to His plan.

Roe v. Wade *did not establish a women's right to choose abortion. It established the right to privacy concerning the abortion procedure and was meant to protect doctors from criminal proceedings.*

At first, I thought it was a cynical comment. Finally, I realized that the truth is far worse than that. Our struggle does not begin and end with abortion. Abortion is just an obvious outcropping of a deep spiritual problem we have as a culture in failing to recognize some of the most fundamental of all biblical truths.

To explain why the Personhood paradigm is much larger than just a plan to end abortion, we first need to understand a bit of history.

Roe v. Wade did not establish a women's right to choose abortion. It established the right to privacy concerning the abortion procedure and was meant to protect doctors from criminal proceedings.

The Personhood of the unborn child is already established in many of our laws. Case in point: Ariel Castro and Charles Van Zant, a Florida state representative from Keystone Heights, has said that *Roe* established a loophole in the law governing murder.

A Brief History of the Recent Pro-Life Movement

At the time *Roe v. Wade* was passed, the only large religious body that had an active plan to oppose abortion was the Roman Catholic Church. Most Protestant denominations were either silent on the issue and some even issued statements of agreement with *Roe*. Now we would expect that from liberal bodies such as the United Methodist Church, the Episcopalian Church, the Evangelical Lutheran Church, the United Church of Christ (Congregationalists), the PCUSA [Presbyterian Church USA]. We expect a weak view on the pro-life issue from the unorthodox—the Seventh Day Adventists, the Unitarians, the Mormons and so on.

Much to our shame, some evangelicals joined the chorus of briefs that were written in favor of *Roe*. Even the conservative Southern Baptist Convention prior to *Roe* called on all Baptists to work for abortion rights....

This complicity in the abortion holocaust is a dark stain on the evangelical movement. It ought to give us cause to pause and consider that evangelicals were in large part responsible for legal abortion.

The Bishop's Plan

The Catholic Bishop's plan was a comprehensive, state-by-state plan to pass a Human Life Amendment at the federal US

Constitutional level, but it also included a grassroots strategy of passing state laws and amendments and using the "states rights" clause of the tenth amendment to resist federal tyranny in the form of legalized child killing.

The Bishops of the Roman Catholic Church, to their great credit, refused to compromise with the "exception clauses" of *Roe* for rape, incest and the health of the mother. Sadly, they didn't have the support of the majority of Americans and especially of the large Protestant church denominations, such as the Southern Baptists, who would not join in an uncompromising, no exceptions stance. The Bishop's Plan failed in part because many state and federal legislators were only willing to support a plan that had the "exceptions." This was the first split in the pro-life movement.

In every state where it has been tried, several "pro-life" organizations . . . have opposed Personhood.

The Hyde Amendment

In 1976, Representative Henry J. Hyde (R-Ill.) sponsored an amendment to the Federal Budget appropriations bill for the Department of Health and Human Services (HHS). His amendment denied Medicaid funding for abortion unless the woman's life is in danger or she is pregnant as a result of rape or incest, but only if the woman reports the incident at the time of its occurrence. Despite opposition from pro-abortion groups, Hyde attached this amendment every year to the same appropriations bill. The Supreme Court has upheld the constitutionality of the Hyde Amendment.

The Hyde Amendment was opposed in the beginning by the Catholic Bishops, since it included the "exceptions," but supported by several evangelical groups who had by now joined the pro-life movement. Although there is evidence that some lives have been saved due to the Hyde Amendment, Personhood advocates worry that any law that allows child murder in certain cases actually strengthens the pro-abortion agenda. It undermines our argument that abortion is child murder. Other life advocates argue that the "exceptions" become a necessity to save some lives even while they "chip away" at *Roe* and try to eliminate abortion incrementally and gradually.

Personhood USA

The modern Personhood movement was begun in the state of Georgia over seven years ago by Georgia Right to Life president Dan Becker. Personhood came about when Becker sought to revive the strategy of the Bishop's Plan focusing on passing a Human Life Amendment to the state constitution of Georgia. Ironically the evangelicals now lined up behind Becker's agenda, while National Right to Life and the Catholic Bishops now opposed it. Their reasoning as I just outlined was that any state law or amendment that did not have the exceptions was unacceptable as a sound strategy to chip away at *Roe*.

In 2008, Personhood USA was then established by Cal Zastrow and Keith Mason, who are now working toward legislative and voter initiatives in over 30 states. In every state where it has been tried, several "pro-life" organizations, including Phyllis Schlafly's Eagle Forum, National Right to Life and the Catholic Bishops have opposed Personhood.

It's ironic that now several conservative "pro-life" commentators, such as Sean Hannity, hold the view that the exceptions are necessary in order to pass restrictive legislation— even though the *Roe* decision was framed around these very exceptions! They want to reverse *Roe* as a decision even while they keep it in place through legislation.

In terms of paradigm shifts, compared to where we were at in 1973, the pro-life movement now stands on its head.

Why Personhood Now?

The shift in the pro-life movement is to go back to square one and define that a human being is a Person from biological beginnings with no exceptions for the circumstances of conception.

The focus of pro-life groups in many countries around the world is shifting from regulating abortion to defining what a Person is.

Already the nation of Mexico, where the capital city recently made abortion legal, about half of the state legislatures have passed Personhood Amendments that would keep the federal government from imposing abortion on the states from above as occurred with *Roe v. Wade* in the United States. In our country, we now have to work backward and pass Personhood even while trying various ways to undo *Roe*. The reality is that we cannot do one without the other. Overturning *Roe* won't make abortion illegal in each state. Passing Personhood won't supersede *Roe*. Now we have two tasks to accomplish at one time.

But this strategy has already worked in Mexico. Poland is moving toward having Personhood in their national constitution. The nation of Hungary has the first constitution of the 21st century. Hungary has the following in their newly written constitution:

"Human dignity is inviolable. Everyone has the right to life and human dignity; the life of a fetus will be protected from conception."

Personhood is a worldwide movement led by the Holy Spirit. The focus of pro-life groups in many countries around the world is shifting from regulating abortion to defining what a Person is.

Pro-life advocates in our own country support Personhood *philosophically* almost without exception. The only difference between Personhood advocates and the rest of the pro-life movement is a disagreement over timing. They want to wait to stack the Supreme Court bench with conservatives and overturn *Roe*. We want a grassroots movement that will vote on Personhood amendments now. I often tell people that if we work toward Personhood now, we will eventually get there. If we delay our obedience, then we will be counted among those who opposed Personhood even when our support was needed the most.

The Biological Time Bomb

There is a biological time bomb ticking. The advances we saw in physics and chemistry in the early 20th century resulted in major paradigm shifts in those sciences. Biology is lagging behind, but huge advances are around the corner. Philosophers and religious leaders have thought about the issues surrounding life, death and immortality for thousands of years, but the structure of the DNA molecule has been known for less than 60 years.

What does that mean? It usually takes a generation or more for a major discovery to percolate through an entire scientific field. The major battles that Personhood advocates will fight in the next 50 years will have nothing to do with abortion. In fact, abortion may all but disappear due to advances in science. In a couple of years, a woman will be able to walk into Walgreens and buy an over-the-counter fertility monitor that may be worn as a watch. This will have the function of telling within a 99.9 percent certainty when the wearer is fertile.

The Promise of Technology

Technology can be used for both good and evil. We should welcome these advances and prepare to use them to save lives. We certainly won't be able to stop the bio-technological tidal wave that is coming. We'll also have scanning devices within the next ten years that will be able to "see" in real time the baby as it develops in the womb—not just during a trip to a doctor—but through an "ultrasound baby monitor" that may be worn at all times just like today's heart monitors.

It is imperative that we seize the opportunity to create cognitive dissonance in the minds of young people who may otherwise think of themselves as pro-choice, perhaps due to the pressure to be politically correct.

Medical technology will be used to save lives in a greater capacity than ever before. Abortion will become increasingly intolerable as a "choice" for women.

However, with this biological time bomb, there is a Pandora's Box of new possibilities that bring serious moral, legal and ethical questions. There is on the horizon the possibility of cloning, genetic engineering, eugenics, embryonic experimentation, organ harvesting, human-animal hybrids, euthanasia, nano-technology, advanced artificial intelligence, "cyborgism," "post-humanism," "trans-humanism," and so on. This might seem like science fiction to you, but if you are part of Generation-Y [individuals born in the early 2000s], you will live to deal with the social conflict these developments in bio-technology will cause.

A Mental Shift

The paradigm shift that we see coming is based on the fact that most pro-choice advocates are actually pro-Personhood once we take the concepts of "anti-abortion" and "pro-life" out of the argument. There is a 50-50 split over the topic of abortion, with many in the "mushy middle" advocating some type of compromise. Over 90 percent of college students interviewed agree that such horrors as eugenics and experimentation on living fetuses ought to be illegal. When they are asked to provide the rationale for their stance, they will often invariably say that this is a developing human being and ought to have the right to dignity.

It is imperative that we seize the opportunity to create cognitive dissonance in the minds of young people who may otherwise think of themselves as pro-choice, perhaps due to the pressure to be politically correct, but are otherwise in favor of Personhood as the only alternative to what they see as Nazi eugenics and other dehumanizing abominations. From there the mental shift to recognizing the full Personhood of the unborn child without exception is just a short step away. . . .

Looking Ahead

Personhood is not about overturning *Roe v. Wade* or even about abortion primarily—we are thinking about sanctity of life issues that are 50 years down the road—and that is how we can win—by recognizing the sanctity of life by defining what a Person is. Personhood is due to the image of God present in all human beings. We are not asking government to define Personhood—we are asking government to recognize it as an inalienable right. . . .

Win or lose, we believe that we will be the winners in the long run because as the Personhood movement gains national attention we will gain the momentum needed to advance in other states, the nation and the world.

Personhood for Eggs Would Have Dangerous Consequences

Kaili Joy Gray

Kaili Joy Gray is a progressive blogger who writes about current events and women's issues from a feminist perspective. Her work currently appears at Wonkette. *Editor's Note: In November 2011, Mississippi voters overwhelmingly rejected Amendment 26, a ballot measure that would have granted the full rights of personhood to fertilized eggs.*

The famous Monty Python song Every Sperm is Sacred is about to become a sad reality in Mississippi. Amendment 26, also known as the Personhood Amendment, is simple on its face: "The term 'person' or 'persons' shall include every human being from the moment of fertilization, cloning or the functional equivalent thereof."

That means a fertilized egg ... would be recognized as a person under this new law, supposedly with all the same rights and protections as the woman who carries it.

The sponsors of this amendment, which will appear on the Nov. 8 ballot this year [2011], and which is expected to pass, are not shy about stating their reasoning for such an amendment: the amendment sets up a direct challenge to *Roe v. Wade* in the hopes of seeing it overturned. If a fertilized egg is legally recognized as a person, the thinking goes, then the destruction of a fertilized egg—whether through abortion or even use of certain types of contraception like the IUD and the morning-after pill, which prevent a fertilized egg from implanting in a woman's uterus—could be recognized as murder, and therefore prosecuted as such.

Church and State

But that's not all the proponents of the bill hope to achieve. Earlier this week, *The New York Times* reported:

> "I view it as transformative," said Brad Prewitt, a lawyer and executive director of the Yes on 26 campaign, which is named for the Mississippi proposition. "Personhood is bigger than just shutting abortion clinics; it's an opportunity for people to say that we're made in the image of God."

Of course, the state has no business making such declarations—that we are made in the image of God—the law of the land. But hardcore believers, like proponents of the Personhood Amendment, seek to destroy the separation between church and state, and they see this amendment as another step in that direction. And of course it would make abortion, contraception and embryonic stem cell research a crime.

At *Slate*, David Plotz and his colleagues posed some semi-tongue-in-cheek questions about the meaning of Personhood for eggs: Can you drink at 20 years and three months? Can you collect Social Security at 64? Would a "dependent embryo" be tax deductible? Would sharing an ultrasound at Facebook be considered child pornography? How does this affect the census?

Already, even without the legal recognition of a fertilized egg as a person, women face interrogation, prosecution and even jail time for the "crime" of miscarrying.

Unknown Consequences

Perhaps *Slate* was just trying to be clever, but the consequences of granting personhood to a fertilized egg are actually unknown. In 2008, when Colorado attempted to pass a personhood amendment, National Public Radio interviewed Professor of Law and Bioethics Jessica Berg on exactly these types of questions:

> [T]he amendment could lead to some bizarre situations—such as counting fertilized eggs in the state census and pregnant drivers using the HOV lanes.

> "If you don't know you're pregnant at that point, and you drink or do something dangerous—or you do something problematic very early on [...] have you committed child abuse and endangerment?" Berg wonders.

> Berg says that as written, the amendment would classify all the fertilized eggs used in fertility labs—which number in the hundreds of thousands—as persons.

> "You could never get rid of them," she says of the fertilized eggs. "It's not clear whether you could freeze them, because we certainly don't have a concept of freezing indefinitely a person. It's not clear how you then adopt them—would you have to go through all the normal adoption proceedings?"

Berg isn't the only one to question what personhood status for fertilized eggs could mean. Other ethicists, lawyers and medical professionals are also at a loss for how to make sense of what fertility specialist Dr. Randall S. Hines describes as "biological ignorance":

> Most fertilized eggs, he said, do not implant in the uterus or develop further.

> "Once you recognize that the majority of fertilized eggs don't become people, then you recognize how absurd this amendment is," Dr. Hines said.

Could Miscarriage Be a Crime?

Yes, the amendment is absurd, but its implications are no laughing matter. Already, even without the legal recognition of a fertilized egg as a person, women face interrogation, prosecution and even jail time for the "crime" of miscarrying.

What happens, then, to women who miscarry under this new law? Will all miscarriages require police reports, trials, prison time, even the death penalty? After all, the majority of people who identify as "pro-life" also support capital punishment, and while they seek to protect fertilized eggs, they have no problem frying those eggs once they're outside the womb.

When voters in Mississippi go to the polls on Nov. 8 to vote on personhood, they'll also be selecting their next governor, but no matter how they vote, they'll end up with a governor who supports this "biological ignorance":

> The Republican candidate, Lt. Gov. Phil Bryant, is co-chairman of Yes on 26 and his campaign distributes bumper stickers for the initiative. The Democratic candidate, Johnny DuPree, the mayor of Hattiesburg and the state's first black major-party candidate for governor in modern times, says he will vote for it though he is worried about its impact on medical care and contraception.

Even opposition from their fellow antichoice allies is no match for the proponents of personhood.

Political Realities

DuPree, by the way, is worried about the impact of the personhood amendment, but apparently, he's a lot more worried about his political future. As Irin Carmon at Salon reports:

> Cristen Hemmins, an anti-26 activist and survivor of a brutal carjacking, rape and shooting, told me she'd gotten a call from Dupree after repeatedly contacting his office. Dupree reiterated that he opposes abortion but thought there should be some provisions for rape and incest victims. Moreover, he said, his daughter had had an ectopic pregnancy and eventually had a child through IVF, both situations potentially impacted by Personhood.
>
> "I said, 'I don't understand, if you're for all these things . . . why are you voting yes?'" Hemmins recalled. "[Dupree] said,

'I'm starting to see that there are issues . . . I've said I'm going to vote yes and it's too late to go back on it now. It'd destroy me politically.'"

It's a pretty sad commentary on the state of affairs in Mississippi when it's considered politically risky to stand up against this kind of insanity. Even some of the staunchest forced birthers, like National Right to Life and the Roman Catholic bishops oppose the Personhood Amendment. Of course, their opposition isn't ideological. They're just afraid it's a poor *tactic* that could backfire and set them back in their ultimate crusade to, yes, outlaw all abortion and birth control.

The Forced-Birth Movement

But even opposition from their fellow antichoice allies is no match for the proponents of personhood. So eager are they to see this amendment succeed in Mississippi, after failing to pass in other states, that, as Robin Marty reported, they came up with a particularly gruesome gimmick to promote their agenda: the "Conceived in Rape" tour. It is, as its name implies, a sick celebration of children whose mothers did not— or, more likely, *could* not—choose to abort rather than carry their rapist's baby to term. Forced birth circuit star Rebecca Kiessling explains at her website, and on tour, that her mother did not abort her when she was impregnated by her rapist because abortion was illegal at the time, and Rebecca is so "hurt" by this knowledge that she is compelled to ensure that all women, like her mother, are denied the right to terminate pregnancies conceived in rape. Rebecca, as an egg, had a *right* to her life; her mother did not.

Monty Python's musical declaration—"*Every sperm is sacred. Every sperm is great. If a sperm is wasted, God gets quite irate.*"—may have been satire, but the proponents of the Personhood Amendment are dead serious.

This is the reality of the War on Women. As the forced birth movement has already been so successful at legislating barriers to abortion access, they are moving on to the next step. It isn't enough for them to take away a woman's right to terminate an unwanted, or even life-threatening, pregnancy. Now they want to take away contraception. They want to criminalize miscarriage. They want to force rape victims to carry their rapists' babies. They want a law that recognizes their interpretation of God and the Bible.

And they want to give legal rights and protections and recognized autonomy to fertilized eggs, as they simultaneously take away rights and protections from the women who carry them.

Legal Abortion Faces Renewed Challenges and Restrictions

Lyle Denniston

Lyle Denniston is the National Constitution Center's adviser on constitutional literacy. He has reported on the US Supreme Court for fifty-five years, currently covering it for SCOTUSblog, an online clearinghouse of information about the Supreme Court's work. Editor's Note: On January 13, 2014, the US Supreme Court declined to hear the Arizona case that sought to revive a state law banning most abortions after twenty weeks of pregnancy based on the argument that a fetus can feel pain.

On January 22, as happens on that day every year, a crowd will gather in front of the Supreme Court to rally against *Roe v. Wade.* Though that ruling establishing a woman's constitutional right to seek an abortion came down nearly forty-one years ago, it remains deeply controversial in America. The efforts to get it overturned, or at least narrowed down, continue unabated.

Long after it became clear that Congress would not send to the states a proposed constitutional amendment to nullify the *Roe* decision, the foes of abortion have found increasingly that they are more likely to have success if they seek restrictions, one state legislature at a time. A wave of new state abortion control laws is just beginning to flow through the inevitable court contests, on the way perhaps to the Supreme Court.

It has been more than six years since the Supreme Court last issued a major ruling on abortion laws. It upheld then a federal law, passed by Congress in 2003, that imposed a nearly total ban on a method known as "partial-birth abortion"—a procedure only used in mid- to late-term abortions. Even though its impact was limited, the ruling gave new energy to the anti-abortion movement, with some of its leaders proclaiming at the time that this decision was the first real sign that *Roe v. Wade* ultimately would be doomed.

A Key Ruling

That ruling, in *Gonzales v. Carhart*, was written by Justice Anthony M. Kennedy who then held—and probably still holds—the deciding vote on abortion issues. It was Kennedy, of course, who in 1992 had helped craft a compromise decision that salvaged most of *Roe v. Wade*, but that also provided new constitutional respect for the life of the developing fetus.

Kennedy's opinion in the partial-birth abortion case enhanced that display of constitutional respect for fetal life. He wrote: "The government may use its voice and its regulatory authority to show its profound respect for the life within the woman."

Some of these laws would forbid abortions after 20 weeks. Laws like that are defended not as a flat ban at that point, but rather as attempts to protect fetuses from feeling pain when an abortion is performed.

Since that ruling, the anti-*Roe* movement has been shifting its strategy away from seeking outright bans on specific methods of abortion, and toward attempts to regulate the circumstances in which terminating pregnancy will be allowed, or forbidden. Much of that strategy is aimed at building upon the protection of the developing fetus, seeing in Kennedy's 2007 opinion an implied invitation to take that specific route.

Beginning with the view that fetal life begins at conception, such laws seek to push earlier into the cycle of pregnancy the point at which a state can step in to protect the fetus. Some of those laws seek to provide fetal protection as early as six weeks into the pregnancy.

Those laws are, of course, a more direct challenge to *Roe*, because they would forbid abortions in the first trimester— the stage in pregnancy where the Supreme Court has provided the most protection for the pregnant woman's choice to terminate. They thus would probably appear, to courts, to be the equivalent of a flat ban, not a mere regulation.

Fetal Pain Laws

But some of these laws would forbid abortions after 20 weeks. Laws like that are defended not as a flat ban at that point, but rather as attempts to protect fetuses from feeling pain when an abortion is performed. Such a law assumes the supposed medical fact that a fetus can begin to feel pain well before the time when the fetus, if born alive, would be viable. Viability has always been the point beyond which state regulatory power would be the greatest, even under the *Roe* decision, but viability is generally assumed not to be possible before about 24 weeks of pregnancy. So, the question arises: can states regulate abortion in a significant way before 24 weeks?

There is physical evidence, the supporters of such laws say, that fetuses can begin to feel pain as early as the sixteenth week, but almost certainly by the twentieth. So the 20-week point has been chosen for such laws as the beginning of state power to regulate to avert fetal pain. Separately, such laws are defended as a form of health regulation for the woman, because of the perceived risks to her of later-term abortion.

Early in 2014, the Supreme Court will be taking its first look at such a 20-week law—one enacted in Arizona in 2012. Arizona is one of thirteen states to take this approach, and a test case involving its statute was the first to reach the Supreme Court.

Arizona officials have gone to considerable lengths, in seeking to put the case before the Supreme Court, to try to show that a 20-week law falls on the regulatory side of abortion control laws, not on the flat ban side. A woman could still seek an abortion beyond twenty weeks, the officials noted, because the Arizona law also allows abortion even beyond twenty weeks if there is a grave risk to the woman's health if the pregnancy were to continue.

Legal Reviews Will Continue

If the Justices accept the case for review, and that could be known before the end of January, that could well be interpreted as a sign that the fetal pain argument was being taken seriously by at least some of the members of the court. But, in a larger sense, that could be taken as a sign that the life of the fetus is going to loom larger in the continued development of the constitutional law of abortion.

The majority that decided in favor of an abortion restriction in 2007 is still intact; the two newest members who have joined the court since then—Justices Elena Kagan and Sonia Sotomayor—probably are not in a position to move the court toward a stance more sympathetic to abortion rights.

If the Arizona case is denied review, that would not be the end of the matter. More of the new abortion control laws are under review in lower federal courts, and some of those may well reach the Supreme Court during 2014. Thus, the constitutional controversy over abortion probably will be an ongoing feature of the year.

Young People Will Shape the Future of Abortion Access

Kate Sheppard

Kate Sheppard was a staff reporter in Mother Jones's *Washington bureau from 2009 to 2013. She is now a senior reporter and the energy and environment editor at* Huffington Post.

Last Tuesday [January 22, 2013] marked the 40th anniversary of *Roe v. Wade*, the Supreme Court decision that affirmed a constitutional right to abortion in the United States. As the case heads into middle age, a new survey from the Pew Forum on Religion & Public Life found that only 44 percent of people between the ages of 18 and 29 could correctly identify what *Roe* was even about.

But survey results like that one only tell part of the story. The fact that many young adults can't correctly identify a particular Supreme Court case shouldn't be taken as a sign that millennials—the generational term commonly used for anyone between the ages of 18 and 30—don't care about reproductive rights. (After all, some of our elected officials can't identify *any* Supreme Court cases.) Millennials' actual beliefs about abortion policy matter more than their ability to identify *Roe*. On that subject, the poll results are clear: 68 percent of 18- to 29-year-olds believe that women should have a right to access abortion—the highest support in any age bracket other than the baby boomers.

The Influence of Millennials

Any group that wants to influence policy in the long run, though, will have to find a way to motivate millennials: There are 80 million of them, and by 2020 they'll make up 40 percent of the voting population. But millennials don't think about reproductive rights in the same way their parents did. Polling by NARAL Pro-Choice America, a top reproductive rights group, has found that although the majority identify as "pro-choice," only about 21 percent are actively advocating for or working on the issue. "It is, in my judgment, a tipping point for this issue," Nancy Keenan, the group's president, told me in an interview earlier this month. "They are pro-choice, but [we need to] connect that to the importance of the political."

The need to engage the next generation of voters on this issue is part of the reason that Keenan, who is 60, announced last year that she is stepping down at NARAL in order to make way for a younger leader. Keenan plans to leave in February, and will be replaced by Ilyse Hogue, who is in her early 40s. "I felt, and my board felt, this was an opportunity, at 40 years of *Roe*, for me to make room for new leadership, and an opportunity for a new leader to engage this generation of millennials," Keenan says.

A number of [Millennials] don't self-identify as "pro-choice," even if they are in practice.

At 36, Kierra Johnson, the executive director of Choice USA, is one of the few leaders of a national reproductive rights group who was born after *Roe*. She shares Keenan's ambitions about connecting with the next generation.

Organizing Young People

Choice USA aims to organize college students to fight for reproductive rights, and to that end, it works with 25 campus groups in six states, including Texas and Kansas, where abortion rights have been under attack in recent years. But it can be tough to organize young people to back a reproductive rights agenda if you don't understand that they're coming at the issue from a new angle, Johnson says. For one, it's harder to get young people fired up about maintaining a right they already have. Compared to an issue like marriage equality, where activists are working proactively *for* something new, reproductive rights groups "have to organize around battles that have technically already been won," Johnson says. "Didn't we already get access to contraception? Didn't we already get access to abortion?" she continued. "It's like, yeah, but . . . either it's been rolled back in some way, or the context has changed."

Another difference, Johnson says, is that many of the young people she works with at Choice USA want to talk about safe sex, positive relationships, or contraception—not abortion. She also finds that a number of them don't self-identify as "pro-choice," even if they are in practice. "In our introductory program, we don't even make people identify as 'pro-choice,'" Johnson says. "Because you lose people. You just have to have an interest, and you have to be open-minded." That's the reasoning behind Planned Parenthood's recent announcement that it, too, is shedding the pro-choice label—a recognition, the group says, of the fact that abortion is an issue where "labels don't reflect the complexity."

Looking Forward

Millennials also seem to like highlighting personal stories about women's experiences with accessing abortion. This is what prompted Advocates for Youth, another reproductive rights group, to launch its "1 in 3 Campaign," a project highlighting the personal stories about abortion. The group bills the campaign, which is based on the statistic that 1 in 3 women will have an abortion at some point in her life, as an effort to move beyond the question of whether abortion should be legal to begin talking about how to reduce its stigma going forward. "Over the next 40 years, we see this generation as the one that will be the linchpin of the abortion access movement," says Julia Reticker-Flynn, manager of the Youth

Activist Network at Advocates for Youth. "Then it was about legality, now it's about access. Even if it's legal, if it's inaccessible, is it really even an option?"

Some worry that a younger generation of activists might take the rights their mothers and aunts and grandmothers won for granted. But that possibility is something to celebrate, Keenan says. "My generation fought so that the next generation of women wouldn't have to worry about this, think about this, care about this," she says. "You could almost say we did our job. They don't think about it because for most of them it is available to them."

That sense of hard-won victory is an opportunity, Choice USA's Johnson says: "I think we're at a place where we have to spend a little less time looking back than looking forward. What about the next 40 years?"

CHAPTER 2

Can Abortion Be Morally Justified?

Chapter Preface

One of the most nuanced issues related to the abortion debate is the question of emergency contraception versus medication abortion. The two things are scientifically quite different, yet there is widespread misunderstanding and frequent disagreement about what each is and does.

Used within seventy-two hours of unprotected sex, emergency contraceptive pills containing the drug levonorgestrel prevent pregnancy by delivering a high dose of the same chemical found in most ordinary birth control pills. Levonorgestrel (often known as "Plan B" because of a brand name) prevents pregnancy by delaying ovulation, interfering with fertilization, or preventing the implantation of a fertilized egg in the uterus. It cannot end an existing pregnancy, but it can keep one from occurring.

In essence, levonorgestrel pills perform the same function as a contraceptive method that has been around since the early 1900s: the IUD (intrauterine device), a small object placed inside the uterus to prevent fertilized eggs from attaching and becoming viable pregnancies. According to a 2002 Dutch study, 60 percent of fertilized eggs never implant and become pregnancies at all, even without contraceptive intervention.

In 2006, the US Food and Drug Administration (FDA) approved levonorgestrel emergency contraceptive pills for nonprescription, over-the-counter sale to adults in the United States; in June 2013, that unrestricted access was extended to all ages.

Medication abortion pills, on the other hand, require the supervision of a doctor, and they work in a very different way—by terminating a fertilized egg that has already implanted in the uterus. Drugs such as mifepristone (also known as RU-486) must be prescribed by a physician and are only permitted for ending early pregnancies of up to forty-nine days. The two-part medication abortion process includes an initial dose of mifepristone to cause the abortion and then a dose of a drug called misoprostol two days later to induce contractions that will expel the embryo.

Available in Europe since 1988, mifepristone was banned for import to the United States for many years, and it took nearly two decades—and lots of controversy—for the FDA to approve its use in 2000. Eleven years later, medication abortions in the United States accounted for 23 percent of all non-hospital abortions and 36 percent of all abortions before nine weeks' gestation, according to data from the Guttmacher Institute, a reproductive rights advocacy organization.

Scientifically speaking, there is a world of difference in how emergency contraceptive pills and medical abortion pills work; one prevents a pregnancy from occurring, while the other ends an already existing pregnancy. That difference lies at the heart of decision-making for many women, who likewise may perceive a moral difference between the two options when considering whether to avoid a pregnancy.

Many people who are strongly religious, however, do not recognize any difference between these drugs because they believe that human life begins at the very moment of fertilization, whether or not the egg ever becomes viable and implants in the uterus. Within such a belief system, emergency contraceptive pills are seen as abortion agents, not contraceptives at all.

Moral objections have led a number of pharmacists around the country to refuse to dispense emergency contraceptives under the protection of so-called conscience laws that excuse medical professionals from performing actions that go against their principles. Such a conflict was also the basis for a federal lawsuit by the Hobby Lobby arts-and-craft store chain, which claimed that being forced to provide its employees with insurance coverage that includes emergency contraceptive drugs (as well as IUDs) under the Affordable Care Act (ACA) violates its religious freedom.

On June 30, 2014, the US Supreme Court ruled that Hobby Lobby and other closely held private companies like it do indeed have the same freedom of religion protections as individuals and can opt out of the ACA's so-called contraceptive mandate on that basis. The ruling, which is expected to have far-reaching consequences, underscores the extent to which personal beliefs about conception and contraception join medical science as cornerstones of today's abortion debate.

The authors in this chapter present a wide variety of views about whether abortion is morally justifiable and if so, under what circumstances, within what parameters, and by what methods.

Safe and Legal Abortion Is a Human Right

Center for Reproductive Rights

The Center for Reproductive Rights is an international advocacy organization that uses the law to advance reproductive freedom as a fundamental human right.

In 2008, an estimated 86 million women had unintended pregnancies. The impact of unintended pregnancies vary immensely depending on such factors as a woman's health, family relationships, economic resources, and the availability of medical care. These and other factors influence her decision to either carry a pregnancy to term or to seek an abortion. Given the complexity of this decision, the only person equipped to make it is the pregnant woman herself.

Governments should respect a woman's human right to make decisions regarding her reproductive life. A woman who decides to have an abortion—as 46 million women do annually—must have access to the facilities and care that will enable her to terminate her pregnancy safely. Governments that prosecute and punish women who have had abortions penalize women for exercising their basic rights. These rights are no less compromised when a woman who decides to terminate a pregnancy can do so only by undertaking a serious risk to her life or health.

International legal support for a woman's right to safe and legal abortion are found in numerous international treaties and other instruments. . . . The right to choose abortion has support in guarantees of life, health, freedom from discrimination, autonomy in reproductive decision-making, freedom from cruel, inhuman, or degrading treatment and the right to enjoy the benefits of scientific progress.

Women's Right to Life

Multiple human rights instruments protect the right to life. In 2000, in elaborating States' obligations in reporting on their compliance with the right to life enshrined in the International Covenant on Civil and Political Rights (ICCPR), the Human Rights Committee called upon States to inform it of "any measures taken by the State to help women prevent unwanted pregnancies, and to ensure that they do not have to undergo life-threatening clandestine abortions."

It is widely acknowledged that in countries in which abortion is restricted by law, women seek abortions clandestinely, often under conditions that are medically unsafe and therefore life-threatening. According to the World Health Organization (WHO), about 21.6 million women had unsafe abortions in 2008. These unsafe abortions were responsible for the deaths of nearly 47,000 women. The incidence of unsafe abortion is closely associated with high maternal mortality rates. Therefore, laws that force women to resort to unsafe procedures infringe upon women's right to life.

The right to health can be interpreted to require governments to take appropriate measures to ensure that women have the necessary information and the ability to make crucial decisions about their reproductive lives.

Several United Nations (UN) human rights bodies have framed maternal deaths due to unsafe abortion as a violation of women's right to life. As a result, they have called on States to review restrictive laws that criminalize abortion and increase access to family planning and sexual and reproductive health information, in order to reduce the number of unsafe abortions.

While the phrase "right to life" has been associated with the campaigns of those who oppose abortion, it has not been interpreted in any international setting to require restrictions on abortion. Most recently, the European Court of Human Rights, in the case *Vo v. France*, ruled that "it is neither desirable, nor even possible as matters stand, to answer in the abstract the question whether the unborn child is a person for the purpose of Article 2 of the Convention . . ." (providing that "[e]veryone's right to life shall be protected by law"). The court therefore refused to adopt a ruling that would have called into question the validity of laws permitting abortion in 39 member states of the Council of Europe.

Women's Right to Health

International law guarantees women the right to "the highest attainable standard of physical and mental health." The right to health requires governments to provide health care and to work toward creating conditions conducive to the enjoyment of good health. In 2000, the Committee on Economic, Social and Cultural Rights recognized that the right to health includes "the right to control one's health and body, including sexual and reproductive freedom, and the right to be free from interference." Furthermore, the right to health "requires the removal of all barriers interfering with access to health services, education and information, including in the area of sexual and reproductive health."

The Protocol to the African Charter on Human and Peoples' Rights on the Rights of Women in Africa (Maputo Protocol) explicitly recognizes that the right to health includes access to safe and legal abortion, at a minimum, in certain circumstances. It requires States Parties to "ensure that the right to health of women, including sexual and reproductive health is respected and promoted" by taking appropriate measures to authorize abortion "in cases of sexual assault, rape, incest, and where the continued pregnancy endangers the mental and physical health of the mother or the life of the mother or the foetus."

Safe Abortion Services Protect Women

The right to health can be interpreted to require governments to take appropriate measures to ensure that women have the necessary information and the ability to make crucial decisions about their reproductive lives, such as determining whether or not to continue a pregnancy, and to guarantee that women are not exposed to the risks of unsafe abortion, which can have devastating effects on their health, leading to long-term disabilities, such as uterine perforation, chronic pelvic pain or pelvic inflammatory disease. Such measures include removing barriers that interfere with women's access to health services, such as legal restrictions on abortion, and ensuring access to high-quality abortion information and services.

Laws that restrict abortion have the effect and purpose of preventing a woman from exercising any of her human rights or fundamental freedoms on a basis of equality with men.

- Several UN human rights bodies have recognized the deleterious impact of restrictive abortion laws on women's health and have consistently raised general concerns about the inaccessibility of safe abortion services.

- The Programme of Action adopted at the International Conference on Population and Development (ICPD) in 1994 called upon governments to consider the consequences of unsafe abortion on women's health. It states that governments should "deal with the health impact of unsafe abortion as a major public health concern."

- At the 1995 Fourth World Conference on Women, the international community reiterated this language and urged governments to "consider reviewing laws containing punitive measures against women who have undergone illegal abortions." In addition, in a paragraph addressing research on women's health, the Platform for Action adopted at this conference urges governments "to understand and better address the determinants and consequences of unsafe abortion."

- In 1999, at the five-year review of the ICPD, governments recognized the need for greater safety and availability of abortion services. They affirmed that "in circumstances where abortion is not against the law, health systems should train and equip health-service providers and should take other measures to ensure that such abortion is safe and accessible. Additional measures should be taken to safeguard women's health."

Women's Right to Equality and Nondiscrimination

The right to gender equality is a fundamental principle of human rights law. All major human rights instruments require freedom from discrimination in the enjoyment of protected human rights. According to the Convention on the Elimination of All Forms of Discrimination against Women, "discrimination against women" includes laws that have either the "effect" or the "purpose" of preventing a woman from exercising any of her human rights or fundamental freedoms on a basis of equality with men. In 1999, the Committee on the Elimination of Discrimination against Women (CEDAW Committee) recognized "laws that criminalize medical procedures only needed by women and that punish women who undergo those procedures" as a barrier to women's access to appropriate health care.

Denying Women Access to Abortion Is a Form of Gender Discrimination

Laws that restrict abortion have the effect and purpose of preventing a woman from exercising any of her human rights or fundamental freedoms on a basis of equality with men.

- Restricting abortion has the *effect* of denying women access to a procedure that may be necessary for their equal enjoyment of the right to health. Only women must live with the physical consequences of unwanted pregnancy. Some women suffer maternity-related injuries, such as hemorrhage or obstructed labor. Women are consequently exposed to health risks not experienced by men.

- Laws that deny access to abortion, whatever their stated objectives, have the *discriminatory purpose* of both denigrating and undermining women's capacity to make responsible decisions about their bodies and their lives. Indeed, it is not surprising that unwillingness to allow women to make decisions about their own bodies often coincides with the tendency to deny women decision-making roles in the areas of political, economic, social, and cultural affairs.

- The CEDAW Committee has consistently expressed concern about restrictive laws that criminalize abortion. Furthermore, the Human Rights Committee has recognized that criminalizing abortion, even in cases of rape, is incompatible with the States' obligation to ensure the equal right of men and women to the civil and political rights set forth in the ICCPR. Additionally, it has indicated that the problem of maternal mortality due to unsafe abortion is evidence of discrimination against women.

Women's Right to Reproductive Self-Determination

Human rights instruments provide the basis for the right of women to make decisions regarding their own bodies. In particular, they require the right to freedom in decision-making about private matters. Such provisions include protections of the right to physical integrity, the right to decide freely and responsibly the number and spacing of one's children and the right to privacy.

The Human Rights Committee has recognized that denying women access to legal abortion services is an arbitrary interference in their private lives.

When a pregnancy is unwanted, its continuation can take a heavy toll on a woman's physical and emotional well-being. Decisions one makes about one's body, particularly one's reproductive capacity, lie squarely in the domain of private decision-making. A pregnant woman may seek advice from others, but only she knows whether she is ready to have a child, and governments should play no role in making that decision for her.

- The Human Rights Committee has recognized that denying women access to legal abortion services is an arbitrary interference in their private lives.

- The European Court of Human Rights has underscored the connection between pregnancy and a woman's private life, which includes her physical and psychological integrity. It has recognized that States have a positive obligation to effectively secure the physical integrity of pregnant women. This obligation requires them to establish procedural safeguards to ensure that women can make an informed decision about whether or not to terminate a pregnancy and access safe and legal abortion services in a timely manner.

Women's Right to Be Free from Cruel, Inhuman, or Degrading Treatment

International law recognizes that women have a right to be free from cruel, inhuman, or degrading treatment. The Human Rights Committee has stated that cruel, inhuman, or degrading treatment is not restricted to acts that cause physical pain, but also applies to mental suffering, which often accompanies denials of access to abortion services.

As a result of restrictive abortion laws and policies, many women experiencing complications of pregnancy and needing therapeutic abortion are forced to suffer from painful, frightening and life-threatening conditions.

Human rights bodies have recognized that restrictive abortion laws can lead to violations of the right to be free from cruel, inhuman and degrading treatment. The Committee against Torture has recognized the impact of restrictive laws, which force women to carry unwanted pregnancies to term or to undergo illegal abortions that often place their health and lives in danger, and noted that the failure of States to take steps to prevent these acts constitutes cruel and inhuman treatment.

The denial of access to abortion services in certain circumstances, regardless of the legality of the procedure, constitutes cruel, inhuman or degrading treatment.

Specifically, it has indicated that a total prohibition on abortion, which forces a woman to carry a pregnancy resulting from a crime of gender-based violence, such as rape, "entails constant exposure to the violation committed against her and causes serious traumatic stress and a risk of long-lasting psychological problems such as anxiety and depression." The Human Rights Committee has stated that criminalizing abortion is incompatible with the right to be free from cruel, inhuman or degrading treatment.

Women Suffer Without Access to Abortion

Women may also undergo severe suffering and anguish when legal abortion services are inaccessible.

In many countries, healthcare personnel refuse to provide legal abortion services because of their own objection or discriminatory attitudes towards abortions. In the case of *L.M.R. v. Argentina*, the Human Rights Committee found that the State's failure to ensure a woman's access to abortion services to which she was legally entitled, caused her physical and mental suffering, which constituted cruel, inhuman or degrading treatment.

Additionally, in the case of *R.R. v. Poland*, the European Court of Human Rights established a violation of the right to be free from inhumane and degrading treatment because of the suffering experienced by R.R., due to the knowledge that she could not terminate her pregnancy even though the fetus had an incurable deformity and she was entitled to have an abortion under the Polish law. The Court stated that "[s]he suffered acute anguish through having to think about how she and her family would be able to ensure the child's welfare, happiness and appropriate long-term medical care."

Furthermore, the denial of access to abortion services in certain circumstances, regardless of the legality of the procedure, constitutes cruel, inhuman or degrading treatment.

In the landmark decision of *K.L. v. Peru*, the Human Rights Committee found that the depression and emotional distress experienced by a 17-year old girl were foreseeable consequences of the State's failure to enable her to benefit from a therapeutic abortion, and constituted a violation of her fundamental right to be free from cruel, inhuman, or degrading treatment. Notably, this ruling did not depend on the legality of abortion.

Women's Right to the Enjoyment of the Benefits of Scientific Progress

The Universal Declaration of Human Rights and the International Covenant on Economic, Social and Cultural Rights enshrine the right to enjoy the benefits of scientific progress.

As the medical and scientific communities make advances in abortion technologies, this right entitles women to access the full range of technologies for the safest abortion care.

The right to the benefits of scientific progress is particularly salient in the context of abortion because numerous safe, effective and low-cost health interventions, such as medical abortions, can substantially improve women's access to safe abortion services, thereby reducing the incidence of unsafe abortion, and decreasing the attendant maternal morbidity and mortality rates. Medical abortion is an alternative to surgical abortion that generally uses two medicines to end a pregnancy. The most common regimen calls for an oral dose of Mifepristone, followed by a dose of Misoprostol up to 48 hours later. This regimen, which can be initiated as soon as pregnancy is confirmed, is approximately 95% effective. In 2005, the WHO added Mifepristone and Misoprostol to its Model List of Essential Medicines, a list intended to guide governments in their prioritization of necessary drugs for budgetary allocations and procurement in their national health systems.

Permitting medical abortion can significantly improve women's overall access to safe abortion because it can be provided in a broad range of settings, such as in practitioner's offices, and can be offered by non-physicians, which helps to expand the pool of providers available to perform safe abortions. Additionally, reducing reliance on physicians can reduce costs and help make abortion more available and accessible to women. By approving medical abortion protocols, training providers and removing barriers to the regimen, governments can ensure that women have access to medical abortion in a safe setting, which allows them to enjoy their right to the benefits of scientific progress.

Most Americans Believe Rape and Incest Justify Abortion

The Associated Press

The Associated Press is a newspaper wire service.

Poll after poll over many years has shown that Americans overwhelmingly support legal access to abortion for women impregnated by rape. Yet the issue remains divisive, as demonstrated by two current rifts—one involving U.S. aid policy overseas, the other highlighting strategy differences within the U.S. anti-abortion movement.

The National Right to Life Committee recently voted to cut ties with one of its most zealous state affiliates, Georgia Right to Life [GRTL]. The move, which angered many anti-abortion activists nationwide, came after the affiliate defied instructions to endorse an anti-abortion bill in Congress because it included exceptions for rape and incest.

Georgia Right to Life's president, Dan Becker, described the March 29 [2014] ouster as "a tragedy" but said his group would stick by its 14-year-old policy of consistently opposing exceptions for rape and incest. "GRTL will stand true to its mission and not be swayed by the prevailing political winds," Becker said.

David O'Steen, executive director of National Right to Life, said his group and Becker's share a long-term goal of eliminating abortion. But short-term, he said, the national group is willing to support legislation that reduces the number of abortions, even if they have rape and incest exceptions.

War and Rape

Meanwhile, a loose coalition of abortion-rights and women's-rights activists is growing increasingly frustrated with President Barack Obama's administration. Despite years of lobbying, the activists have failed to persuade Obama to issue an executive order stipulating that U.S. foreign aid—though prohibited by Congress from subsidizing abortions as a method of family planning—could be used to provide abortions for women raped in wars.

The New York-based Global Justice Center, leading the push for an executive order, says many thousands of woman have been impregnated by rapists during recent conflicts in Rwanda, Bosnia, Congo, Syria and elsewhere, and yet most major international humanitarian organizations balk at offering abortions for fear of jeopardizing their U.S. funding.

"Since the U.S. is the largest humanitarian aid donor, its abortion ban has become the de facto policy in most war zones where rape is used as a weapon of war," said the center's legal director, Akila Radhakrishnan.

Asked about the issue, the White House press office referred The Associated Press to the National Security Council, which advises the president on foreign policy matters. Two days later, the NSC said it was declining to comment.

Clear Public Opinion

The two controversies are notable in part because the American public is not closely divided on the issue of abortion access for rape victims. National polls taken since the 1970s consistently have shown that at least 70 percent of Americans support such access, and less than 25 percent oppose it.

You have to deal with the reality of the social and political climate.

O'Steen, the National Right to Life leader, acknowledged the polling results in a written analysis of the 2012 election.

"An overwhelming majority believes abortion should be allowed for rape," he wrote. "If that is the issue that defines what it means to be pro-choice or pro-life, then a majority will side with the pro-choice label."

In a telephone interview, O'Steen stressed that National Right to Life "doesn't want any child conceived by rape or incest to be killed by abortion." But that outlook, he said, does not prevent his group from endorsing certain anti-abortion bills that include the rape exception.

"We want to save all the lives that we can," he said. "You have to deal with the reality of the social and political climate."

National Right to Life's break with the Georgia group dismayed some anti-abortion activists, among them Keith Mason, co-founder of the Personhood USA movement that supports legislation defining human life as beginning at conception.

"What message does it send to our pro-life representatives when you whip them to support legislation that denies the right to life to innocent babies conceived in rape?" Mason said in a statement.

A Movement Divided

The president of National Right to Life's Ohio affiliate, Mike Gonidakis of Ohio Right to Life, also opposed the ouster of Georgia Right to Life. He said the airing of differences over rape and incest exceptions was harmful to the anti-abortion movement and suggested it would be wiser to focus on approaches that have broader public support, such as restricting late-term abortions.

"I struggle when I hear members of the pro-life community argue about rape and incest exceptions," he said. "I'm not saying give up on it, but let's fight the battles we can win."

Michael New, a political science professor at the University of Michigan-Dearborn, said the anti-abortion movement could be harmed if friction worsened between those favoring an incremental approach and those with an absolutist outlook. "The risk is that when elected officials see a lot of intense disagreement among like-minded groups, they tend to sit back and do nothing," rather than alienate one faction or the other, New said.

Internationally, the campaign to increase abortion access for wartime rape victims has made some progress. Political leaders in Britain, Norway and the Netherlands have supported it, as has U.N Secretary General Ban Ki-moon, who last year endorsed "access to safe emergency contraception and services for the termination of pregnancies resulting from rape."

Twice during 2013, the U.N. Security Council—including the United States—passed resolutions calling for a full range of sexual and reproductive health services to be made available to women victimized by sexual violence.

The Global Justice Center contends that omitting the option of abortion from the medical treatment provided to women raped in war violates their rights under the Geneva Conventions that protect war victims.

Although the word "abortion" did not appear in the text of the resolutions, it was clear that the procedure was at issue, as evidenced in the opposition expressed by the Vatican's U.N. observer, Archbishop Francis Chullikatt.

"The death of innocent unborn children only visits further violence on women already in difficulty," he said.

Abortion and the Geneva Conventions

The Global Justice Center contends that omitting the option of abortion from the medical treatment provided to women raped in war violates their rights under the Geneva Conventions that protect war victims.

"Within three days of taking office, President Obama affirmed that the U.S. would fully support the rights of military detainees under Geneva Conventions," said the center's president Janet Benshoof. "Yet, after five years, the president continues to turn a blind eye to ending the suffering of women victims of war who are forced to bear the children of their rapists, in large part due to the U.S. abortion ban."

The center says many of the rape victims in armed conflicts are minors, with bodies not developed enough to safely bear children. Without the option of safe, legal abortion, says the center, these victims face a high risk of death from illegal abortion, suicide or childbearing.

Doctors Without Borders, which has a policy of accepting no U.S. government funds, is one of the few major international humanitarian organizations with an explicit policy of providing abortions in cases where its doctors feel that's appropriate.

"We have seen time and time again that in the absence of safe abortion care, women will seek to terminate an unwanted pregnancy by other means, and unsafe abortions very often lead to more suffering and even death," the organization said in an email.

Severe Fetal Defects Justify Late-Term Abortion

Jennifer Massoni

Jennifer Massoni is a longtime writer and magazine editor who is currently at work on a memoir, Lorenzo's Heart: The Anatomy of a Decision, *which chronicles her and her husband's decision to terminate her pregnancy because her unborn baby, Lorenzo, had a fatal heart defect.*

For the past year, I've tried not to get political in this space, as I grieve Lorenzo and do my best to honor his short physical existence and eternal significance.

I can no longer do so.

Earlier this week, the House of Representatives passed an unconsitutional bill banning abortion after 20 weeks post-fertilization (22 weeks including pre-fertilization). *The New York Times* said "the bill is a violation of Supreme Court precedent. The court has ruled that women have a right to an abortion until the fetus could live outside the womb, generally starting around 24 weeks of pregnancy." But states have been violating this precedent for the past two years, evidence that our constitutional reproductive rights are under real threat. Why aren't we standing up and defending these rights as passionately as members of the NRA [National Rifle Association] are defending our Second Amendment rights? As Judy Nicastro wrote in her *New York Times* op-ed yesterday [June 20, 2013] about her termination at 23 weeks due to her child's unlikely survival outside the womb, this is "part of a trend toward restricting second- and even first-trimester abortions.

Ten states have banned most abortions after 20 or 22 weeks; Arkansas, after 12, and North Dakota, after 6."

While these laws may be challenged, and while President [Barack] Obama has said he won't sign this bill into law, as it "shows contempt for women's health and rights" (*New York Times*), the scary reality is that they reflect a mass effort to whittle away hard-earned reproductive rights that women have had for over 40 years. That is the big picture. When we take a more personal view (and trust me, every choice is personal), we see the painful consequences of a bill like this passing. If it were to become law under different leadership, the general public likely wouldn't realize the difference two weeks can make. Allow me to tell you just what a difference it would make.

A Heartbreaking Discovery

My son's fatal heart defect, Hypoplastic Left Heart Syndrome (HLHS), was not detected until my 23rd week of pregnancy. When Ryan and I were told that Lorenzo had only two chambers instead of four, our own hearts were cut in half. We acted fast. Within 48 hours, we were on a plane home to California to seek second opinions. Neither our minds nor our hearts were in any way made up about what we would do for our son, whom we wanted more than anything in the world.

I wonder who in Washington actually thinks anyone wants an abortion, much less a second-trimester abortion.

Five days elapsed from the time we heard the words "the heart does not look normal" to when I held my lifeless son in my arms, after choosing to prevent his suffering while he was still safe and warm inside me. I made a subsequent choice, choosing to deliver his body into our world, giving him a dignity in death I would not have been able to give him life. This experience came down to a matter of days as well as a matter of measurement because while I was nearly 24 weeks pregnant, my son was measuring closer to 22 weeks. We'll never know for sure, but I can surmise that his heart was already slowing his growth.

A Painful and Personal Decision

I can likely never fully explain to you why we made the choice we did. The politicians who debated in Congress talked about the sanctity of life, as if women in my position do not believe in that sanctity. Let me tell you that I believe in it so strongly that I did not want the being Ryan and I created out of love to be subjected to near constant pain, discomfort, confusion, and fear in an effort to prolong his life. How do you explain to a baby why he is being poked and prodded all day long? How does he understand multiple open-heart surgeries over his first two years of life, if he's "lucky" enough to survive that long? How do you prepare him to die? Did you know that the NICU [neo-natal intensive care unit] prescribes anti-anxiety medication to these infants as they are being treated for the host of complications that arise when half a heart begins to ravage a tiny body? Imagine your newborn child also confronting anxiety as he battles infection, bleeds, blood clots, strokes, as he requires oxygen and vomits formula because his body can't process it, as he eventually eats only breast milk at one year old, weighing only 12 pounds.

Bravery Takes Many Forms

I wonder who in Washington imagined this on Tuesday. I wonder who in Washington actually thinks anyone wants an abortion, much less a second-trimester abortion. If you are a mother having to terminate in the second trimester, it is because your child is going to face such unimaginable suffering you cannot imagine putting him through it. It's because your own life is in jeopardy. It's because you are brave enough to let go of all of your dreams in order to spare another life. Yes, I call it bravery, just as I call it brave for any mother to carry a fatally ill child to term and care for that child through all of his days, no matter how little they are. All of it is as brave as it is heartbreaking, something that is not being acknowledged by this bill.

A Misguided Bill

The bill's premise is one of pain, "based on the medically disputed theory that fetuses can feel pain" (HuffPo) [Huffington Post] after 22 weeks. Why are politicians acting like doctors? Especially over disputed theories? Why are they allowed to? What prompted this when the country is facing so many other problems? House Republicans (women account for only 19 out of 234) "argued that the bill was necessary in light of the case of Kermit Gosnell, a Philidelphia abortion provider who was recently convicted of murder for providing late-term abortions" (HuffPo). I am just as horrified by that man's actions as Congress is, and justice should be served for the lives he took. It's despicable, but it's my understanding that he was performing those atrocities on healthy babies after 24 weeks, the current legal limit for a termination. A two-week change in the law would not have saved those babies, but for a parent carrying a terminally-ill child, it can make a world of difference.

I am grateful for that hour with Lorenzo, and I am grateful that we could act on our son's behalf within the confines of the law.

I would like to tell those politicians that pain was at the basis of our decision as well. It was the first question I asked about Lorenzo fighting his disease, and it was the first question I asked when we made our decision to spare him that fight: Would it hurt him? The head of gynecology at one of the top medical institutions in the world assured me that it wouldn't. There would be a shot of medicine into my amniotic fluid. He would be untouched. He would go to sleep. All the pain would be mine and Ryan's.

Were this bill law last June, Ryan and I wouldn't have been able to do what we did—out of love—to prevent Lorenzo's pain. We would have been legally bound to bring him into our world even though his heart was not designed to survive in it. We would then have been ethically and legally obligated to perform countless surgeries to prolong physical life, but I am sorry, not the quality or sanctity of that life. And we would have done so with all the love in our hearts and all the pain in seeing him suffer.

Grateful for Choice

When I held my son, his face was at peace. There was no grimace, no evidence of struggle. Again, all of that was happening on my face as I sobbed in awe at my child and on Ryan's as he sat stunned next to us. Lorenzo's was as beautiful and serene a face as I could ever imagine laying eyes upon. I am grateful for that hour with Lorenzo, and I am grateful that we could act on our son's behalf within the confines of the law.

Thank you for listening. I don't expect all of you to agree with me, but I do expect all of us to consider the consequences of these bills as they pass. Still, I worry all of our minds are made up on these issues—abortion, gun control. What does it take to change a mind? To sway a heart? Usually, a massacre, a tragedy, a Sandy Hook. In my world, the tragedy happened the day I learned my son wouldn't survive long in our world. The added tragedy would have been having no choice but to make him live a shortened, painful life and knowing there had been a time, recently in our country, when his father and I could have prevented it.

Abortion Can Never Be Morally Justified

American Life League

Founded in 1979, American Life League is the country's largest grassroots Catholic pro-life education organization. The non-profit group is committed to protecting the lives of all human beings from the moment of conception to their natural death.

The idea of a total ban on all abortions makes some people uncomfortable. After all, we've been told for years that there are situations in which abortion, though a poor choice, is the best option. That, however, is untrue. Abortion always claims a human person's life, and therefore is never an appropriate choice.

The "big lie" theory says if an untrue statement is repeated often enough, the people will start to accept it as truth. Such is the case with the erroneous mantra that abortion must be permitted in cases of rape, incest, fetal deformity and threat to the mother's life.

Rape and incest are similar in the sense that both are criminal acts. In our system of justice, we punish the criminal. We do not punish the victim, nor do we punish the criminal's children. We are told, however, that if pregnancy occurs as a result of rape or incest, offering the victim an abortion is the compassionate thing to do. No woman should be "forced to carry that monster's child," we are told.

Abortion Retraumatizes Women

The trauma of sexual assault is very real, and there is no intention here to downplay that. Abortion carries its own variety of trauma, however; women—even those who were victims of sexual assault—have reported years of physical, emotional and psychological difficulty following their abortions. Abortion did not solve their problem; it merely created additional ones.

There is also the very important fact that abortion takes the life of a living human being. The circumstances of conception may have been criminal, but the life of the newly-created human being is just as valuable as any other person's. We do not put criminals' innocent children to death in our culture; it simply isn't done. It should not be done in this situation, either.

Fetal Abnormality

Expectant parents can treat a diagnosis of fetal deformity or other form of birth defect almost as if it were death itself. It is not a physical death, but a death of hopes and dreams. Visions of a "normal" childhood—playing games, going to school, growing up and starting families of their own—vanish in a flash. Parents in this moment of despair are often told they should simply go ahead and terminate the pregnancy and get on with their lives.

If the pregnancy is threatening the mother's life, it would seem that lethal force—an abortion—would be a permissible form of self-defense. . . . It sounds like a good argument, but it simply isn't true.

The first problem here is that medical opinions can be just that—opinions. There are countless cases of parents who permitted their children to live and found out at birth that the experts were wrong. Also, imagine the horror of the parents who abort their child, only to see that they had destroyed a perfect baby. That is simply too difficult to comprehend.

Abortions in case of fetal abnormality, however, are just like all other abortions. They take the lives of innocent human beings. Abortions in these cases raise frightening prospects, for if it is all right to kill a disabled person in the womb, could it one day be considered permissible to kill a disabled infant? A disabled adult? The answer is clearly "no" in those cases; why is there any question when the victim is a child in the womb?

The Mother's Life

This excuse for allowing abortion sounds reasonable. If the pregnancy is threatening the mother's life, it would seem that lethal force—an abortion—would be a permissible form of self-defense. The child is not really "attacking" the other, but his presence puts her at risk. It sounds like a good argument, but it simply isn't true.

Hundreds of doctors have signed a statement that puts the situation in perspective. The statement reads, "There is never a situation in the law or in the ethical practice of medicine where a preborn child's life need be intentionally destroyed by procured abortion for the purpose of saving the life of the mother. A physician must do everything possible to save the lives of both of his patients, mother and child. He must never intend the death of either."

A tubal (or ectopic) pregnancy, for instance, can indeed be life-threatening. But the treatment, even if it is fatal to the child, is not a "procured abortion." The doctor wants to save the baby, but knows that is unlikely. The baby's death is an unintended consequence of the physician's effort to save the mother. There are similar cases involving the treatment of cancer in which the baby's death can be an unintended consequence. But again, these are medical treatments, not abortion.

Direct Versus Indirect Abortion

It is important to distinguish between direct abortion, which is the intentional and willed destruction of a preborn child, and a legitimate treatment a pregnant mother may choose to save her life. Operations that are performed to save the life of the mother—such as the removal of a cancerous uterus or an ectopic pregnancy that poses the threat of imminent death— are considered indirect abortions.

They are justified under a concept called the "principle of double effect." Under this principle, the death of the child is an unintended effect of an operation independently justified by the necessity of saving the mother's life.

Essentially, both mother and child should be treated as patients. A doctor should try to protect both. However, in the course of treating a woman, if her child dies, that is not considered abortion.

"Today it is possible for almost any patient to be brought through pregnancy alive, unless she suffers from a fatal disease such as cancer or leukemia, and if so, abortion would be unlikely to prolong, much less save the life of the mother."

–Alan Guttmacher, former Planned Parenthood president

"There are no conceivable clinical situations today where abortion is necessary to save the life of the mother. In fact, if her health is threatened and an abortion is performed, the abortion increases risks the mother will incur regarding her health."

–Dr. Bernard Nathanson, American Bioethics Advisory Commission

There is only one purpose for abortion—ending the life of the child. The "life of the mother" situation for abortion is simply bogus.

The Rights of a Woman Do Not Outweigh the Rights of a Child

AbortionFacts.com

AbortionFacts.com is a nonprofit Christian pro-life education organization.

The comparison between a baby's rights and a mother's rights is unequal. What is at stake in abortion is the mother's lifestyle, as opposed to the baby's life. Therefore, it is reasonable for society to expect an adult to live temporarily with an inconvenience if the only alternative is killing a child.

Of course a child does not have more rights than her mother. Any two people are equal, and any two people have equal rights. Hence, a mother has every bit as much right to live as any child. But in nearly all abortions, the woman's right to live is not an issue, because her life is not in danger.

The mother has not only the right to live, but also the right to the lifestyle of her choice—as long as that choice does not rob other people of even more fundamental rights, the most basic of which is the right to live. The right to a certain lifestyle is never absolute and unconditional. It is always governed by its effects on others.

Planned Parenthood states: The desire to complete school or to continue working are common reasons women give for choosing to abort an unplanned pregnancy.

Completing school and working are desirable things in many cases, and pregnancy can make them difficult. But a woman normally can continue school and work during pregnancy. If she gives up a child for adoption, she need not give up school or work. If she chooses to raise the child herself, there are childcare options available if she must work outside the home. I am not suggesting this is ideal, nor do I say it callously. I have worked with single mothers and know their difficulties. I am simply pointing out there are alternatives, any one of which is preferable to an innocent child's death.

Regardless of the challenges, one person's right to a preferred lifestyle is not greater than another person's right to a life.

Judith Jarvis Thomson's Defense of Abortion

Abortion-rights advocate Judith Jarvis Thomson invented an analogy that has been widely quoted in pro-choice literature and debates. She compares pregnancy to a situation in which someone wakes up strapped to a famous but unconscious violinist. Imagine, Thomson says, that some group called the Society of Music Lovers has "kidnapped" you because you have a certain blood type. Now you are being forced to stay "plugged in" to the violinist's body for nine months until he is viable, or able to live on his own.

Over 99% of all pregnancies are the result of sexual relations in which both partners have willingly participated.

Thomson then asks what if it were not just nine months, but nine years or considerably longer? (Apparently this is a comparison to having to raise a child once he is born.) Thomson assumes that readers would find such a situation "outrageous" and would not consider it their obligation to be subjected to nine months—at least—of bondage and misery for the sake of the violinist, who is little more than a human parasite.

This analogy is worth a closer examination, both because of its popularity and because it is typical of the way the abortion issue is framed by pro-choice advocates. Here are six fallacies of this argument that cut to the heart of the abortion debate:

Rebuttal #1: Over 99% of all pregnancies are the result of sexual relations in which both partners have willingly participated.

One is rarely coerced into pregnancy. Though pro-lifers may be in Thomson's mind, neither they nor anyone else is parallel to the Society of Music Lovers. No one is going around forcing people to get pregnant. The outrage the reader feels at the idea of being kidnapped and coerced is an effective emotional device, but it is a distortion of reality.

Rebuttal #2: Pregnancy is a much different experience than the analogy depicts.

Pregnancy is portrayed as a condition in which one is unable to leave the room, to socialize, to have a job, or even to get out of bed. Carrying a child is depicted as a horrid, degrading, and debilitating situation. Both medical science and the personal experience of millions of women argue against this bleak and twisted picture. Carrying a child is a natural condition in which there is some inconvenience. But few women are bedridden during their pregnancies. Most are socially active, capable of working, traveling, and exercising almost to the day the child is delivered.

Rebuttal #3: Even when pregnancy is unwanted or difficult, it is a temporary condition.

Since the great majority of abortions take place from seven weeks to six months of development, the actual difference between the woman who aborts her child and the woman who doesn't is not nine months but three to seven months. The analogy to nine years or even a lifetime of being chained to someone is obviously invalid since after birth a woman is free to give up her child to one of the hundreds of thousands of families waiting to adopt infants in this country. While pregnancy is a temporary condition, abortion produces a permanent condition—the death of a child.

Rebuttal #4: In this scenario, mother and child are pitted against each other as enemies.

The mother is at best merely a life-support system and at worst the victim of a crime. The child is a leech, a parasite unfairly taking advantage of the mother. Love, compassion, and care are nowhere present. The bonding between mother and child is totally ignored. The picture of a woman waking up in a bed, strapped to a strange unconscious man is bizarre and degrading to women, whose pregnancy and motherhood are natural.

Rebuttal #5: The child's presence during pregnancy is rarely more inconvenient than his presence after birth.

[The] argument for abortion is based in utilitarianism, the idea that whatever brings a person momentary happiness or relief is the right course of action.

The burden of a born child is usually greater on a woman than the burden of an unborn. Yet if a parent of a two-year-old decides that she is tired of being a parent and that no one has the right to expect her to be one any longer, society nonetheless recognizes that she has certain responsibilities toward that child. She can surrender him for foster care or adoption, but she cannot abuse, neglect, or kill the child. If the solution to the stresses of pregnancy is killing the preborn child, is killing not also the solution to the stresses of parenting the preschooler?

Rebuttal #6: Even when there is no felt obligation, there is sometimes real obligation.

If a woman is being raped or murdered, what do we think of those who make no effort to rescue the woman? Don't we recognize that there is moral responsibility toward saving a life, even if it involves an inconvenience or risk we did not ask for or want? For the woman carrying a child, isn't it a significant consideration that her own mother made the same sacrifice for her? Can we forget that every one of us was once that "leech," that "parasite," that "violinist" dependent on our mothers in order to live? Aren't you glad your mother looked at pregnancy—and looked at you—differently than portrayed by this pro-choice analogy? This argument for abortion is based in utilitarianism, the idea that whatever brings a person momentary happiness or relief is the right course of action. This is a shaky foundation for any society that hopes to be moral and just in its treatment of the weak and needy.

In this Alice-in-Wonderland approach, one's choice is not made in light of scientific and moral realities. One's choice is itself the only important reality, overshadowing all matters of fact.

Human Beings Have the Right to Live

See if you can spot what's wrong with the following statement: "Even if the unborn are human beings, they have fewer rights than the woman. No one should be expected to donate her body as a life-support system for someone else."

Does this sound reasonable at first glance? WAIT! . . .

Once we grant that the unborn are human beings, it should settle the question of their right to live.

One pro-choice advocate, in the face of the overwhelming evidence, admitted to me that the unborn are human beings. He then added, "But that's irrelevant to the issue of a woman's right to have an abortion." But how can one's humanity be irrelevant to the question of whether someone has the right to kill him? Wasn't the black person's humanity relevant to the issue of slavery, or the Jew's humanity relevant to the ethics of the Holocaust? Not only is the unborn's humanity relevant, it is the single most relevant issue in the whole abortion debate.

In the *Roe v. Wade* decision, Justice Harry Blackmun stated: "We need not resolve the difficult question of when life begins."

In fact, this question is not difficult at all, as the many scientists quoted under fact #1 attest. But no matter what answer we come to, isn't the question of whether living children are being killed by abortion precisely the question we must resolve?

Writing in the *New York Times*, pro-choice Barbara Ehrenreich says: "A woman may think of her fetus as a person or as just cells depending on whether the pregnancy is wanted or not. This does not reflect moral confusion, but choice in action."

Moral Relevatism

In this Alice-in-Wonderland approach, one's choice is not made in light of scientific and moral realities. One's choice is itself the only important reality, overshadowing all matters of fact. But if society operated this way, every killing of a person would be justifiable. The real issue would not be the worth of the person killed, but the free choice of the one doing the killing. If a man doesn't want his wife, he can think of her as a nonperson. If he chooses to kill her, it would not be "moral confusion," but "choice in action."

Ms. Ehrenreich goes on to say: "Moreover, a woman may think of the fetus as a person and still find it necessary and morally responsible to have an abortion."

We must not miss the implications of this viewpoint. It says that one may acknowledge the personhood of a fellow human being, yet feel that for one's personal benefit it is legitimate—even "morally responsible"—to kill that other person. Though this is a logical conclusion of abortion-rights thinking, if carried out in our society it would ultimately mean the end of all human rights and social justice.

The Wanted and the Unwanted

Naomi Wolf admits that her fellow feminists have lied to themselves in depersonalizing and dehumanizing the unborn:

> This has led to a bizarre bifurcation in the way we who are prochoice tend to think about wanted as opposed to unwanted fetuses: the unwanted ones are still seen in schematic black-and-white drawings while the wanted ones have metamorphosed into vivid and moving color. Even while [former surgeon general Joycelyn] Elders spoke of our need to "get over" our love affair with the unwelcome fetus, an entire growth industry—Mozart for your belly; framed sonogram photos; home fetal-heartbeat stethoscopes—is devoted to sparking fetal love affairs in other circumstances, and aimed especially at the hearts of over-scheduled yuppies. If we avidly cultivate love for the ones we bring to term, and "get over" our love for the ones we don't, do we not risk developing a hydroponic view of babies—and turn them into a product we can cull for our convenience?

> Any happy couple with a wanted pregnancy and a copy of *What to Expect When You're Expecting* can see the cute, detailed drawings of the fetus whom the book's owner presumably is not going to abort, and can read the excited descriptions of what that fetus can do and feel, month by month. Anyone who has had a sonogram during pregnancy knows perfectly well that the 4-month-old fetus responds to outside stimulus—"Let's get him to look this way," the technician will say, poking gently at the belly of a delighted mother-to-be. *The Well Baby Book*, the kind of whole-grain holistic guide to pregnancy and childbirth that would find its audience among the very demographic that is most solidly prochoice reminds us that: "Increasing knowledge is increasing the awe and respect we have for the unborn baby and is causing us to regard the unborn baby as a real person long before birth. . . ."

> So, what will it be: Wanted fetuses are charming, complex REM-dreaming little beings whose profile on the sonogram

looks just like Daddy, but unwanted ones are mere "uterine material"? How can we charge that it is vile and repulsive for prolifers to brandish vile and repulsive images if the images are real? To insist that the truth is in poor taste is the very height of hypocrisy.

In reality, outlawing abortion wouldn't be giving unborn children more rights, it would simply gain for them the one most fundamental right that no one can live without, the right to life.

"The height of hypocrisy" is one feminist's appraisal of this double standard. Yet, amazingly, in this same essay Wolf still defends abortion, saying it should be done with grief and mourning for the loss of the child. In some ways, her bottom-line message is even more frightening. She is telling people: "Stop lying to yourselves about the unborn ... these are real babies, just as real and just as precious when we don't want them as when we do. Keep that tragic fact in mind as you go ahead and kill them."

Babies Have the Right Not to Be Killed

Some have suggested that prohibiting a woman from having an abortion is to place the value of an embryo or fetus above that of the woman herself. Restricting abortion does not imply that the child is more valuable than the mother. Rather, it recognizes that the child's right to not be killed is more fundamental than the woman's right to not be pregnant.

Politically speaking, abortion is an issue that involves competing rights. On the one hand, you have the mother's right not to be pregnant. On the other hand, you have the baby's right not to be killed. The question that must be answered is this. Which right is more fundamental? Which right has a greater claim? Abortion advocates argue that outlawing abortion would, in essence, elevate the rights of the unborn over and above those of the mother. "How can you make a fetus more important than a grown woman?", they might ask. In reality, outlawing abortion wouldn't be giving unborn children more rights, it would simply gain for them the one most fundamental right that no one can live without, the right to life.

Pregnanacy Is Temporary but Abortion Is Permanent

If a baby is not to be aborted, then the pregnant mother must remain pregnant. This will also require of her sickness, fatigue, reduced mobility, an enlarged body, and a new wardrobe. Fortunately, it is not a permanent condition. On the flip side, for a pregnant woman not to be pregnant, her child must be killed (unless she is past her 21st week of pregnancy, in which case the baby may well survive outside the womb). Abortion costs the unborn child his or her very life and it is a thoroughly permanent condition. This is what's at stake, both for the child and for the mother. It is not an issue of who is more important, but rather who has more on the line.

Any time the rights of two people stand in opposition to each other, the law exists to protect the more fundamental right. We see this all the time. For example, if a car is driving down a street while someone is crossing that street, the law requires the driver of the car to slow down and stop (giving up their right to drive where they want, when they want, and at what speed they want) so that the pedestrian may cross the street in front of him. Why? Why must the driver temporarily give up his right to drive down the street just because someone else is walking across the street? Why is the right of the man on foot upheld while the right of the man in the car is denied?

Less Fundamental Rights Must Yield

It is not because the pedestrian is more valuable than the driver but rather because, if the driver doesn't stop, the pedestrian will likely be killed. In order for the driver to proceed down the street at full speed, at that moment, it will cost the pedestrian his life. In order for the pedestrian to finish crossing the street, at that moment, it will cost the driver a few minutes of drive time. The autonomy of the driver must be temporarily suspended to protect the life of the pedestrian. Though a pregnant woman gives up far more than a few minutes of drive time, she gives up far less than the baby, who would otherwise be killed.

At a basic level, the driver/pedestrian example helps illustrate how the law should respond when the rights of individuals conflict with each other. Namely, the less fundamental rights must yield to the more fundamental rights.

The comparison between a baby's rights and a mother's rights is unequal. What is at stake in abortion is the mother's lifestyle, as opposed to the baby's life. Therefore, it is reasonable for society to expect an adult to live temporarily with an inconvenience if the only alternative is killing a child.

Late-Term Abortion
Is Infanticide

Mary L. Davenport

Mary L. Davenport is an obstetrician-gynecologist who practices in El Sobrante, California.

In the aftermath of the killing of George Tiller, the Kansas abortionist, on May 31, 2009, we have heard praises of his compassion and courage in performing late-term abortions. According to NARAL Pro-Choice Colorado, "Dr. Tiller was one of few doctors with the expertise necessary to provide safe, professional abortions under the most difficult of circumstances: when a woman who had wanted children was told late in her pregnancy that a severe fetal anomaly had developed or that continuing the pregnancy threatened her own life." Former patients gave heart-wrenching testimonies of late-term abortion being their only alternative upon discovery of fatal birth defects. In his clinic's video given to late-term abortion patients, Tiller welcomed women who came to him to "end a pregnancy early because of some serious disease process: cancer, lymphoma, diabetes, high blood pressure, heart disease," as well as those who were bearing children with fetal anomalies. The president of the Center for Reproductive Rights, a legal advocacy organization, claimed that the closing of Tiller's clinic left "an immediate and immense void in the availability of abortion."

But is late-term abortion (or any abortion) ever really necessary? Does the demise of a clinic performing late-term abortions leave a "void" that is harmful to women?

Defining Late-Term Abortion

The Tiller murder and the legislative and judicial hearings on partial-birth abortion have focused public attention on late-term abortion in the U.S. Late-term abortion is not an exact medical term, but it has been used to refer to abortions in the third trimester (28–39 weeks) or even second trimester abortions (13–27 weeks). According to less-than-perfect statistics collected by the Centers for Disease Control (CDC) and the Guttmacher Institute, 12% of U.S. abortions, approximately 144,000 procedures a year, are performed after the first trimester, that is, more than 12 weeks elapsed time after the woman's last menstrual period. About 15,600 abortions, 1.3% of the 1.2 million abortions in 2005, occur after the 20th week.

Late-term abortions have been part of the American landscape since the Supreme Court issued its landmark 1973 rulings in *Roe v. Wade* and *Doe v. Bolton*—both issued on the same day. Roe authorized abortion beyond the point of fetal viability to protect the "life or health" of the mother. Doe provided such a broad definition of "health" that it effectively required that there be abortion-on-demand through a pregnancy's entirety. Thus, the Supreme Court's abortion decisions imposed on the United States one of the most permissive abortion law regimes in the world.

Intentional abortion for maternal health, particularly after viability, is one of the great deceptions used to justify all abortion.

Although the reproductive health pioneer, Dr. Elizabeth B. Connell, predicted in 1971 that contraception and early abortion would render late-term abortion obsolete, joining "the bubonic plague and poliomyelitis as practically historic conditions," the proportion of late-term abortions has varied little in the last two decades. Ron Fitzsimmons, executive director of the National Coalition of Abortion Providers, shocked the general public in 1997 when he admitted that the vast majority of partial-birth abortions were performed on healthy mothers and babies. Contrary to the assertion of abortion rights supporters that late-term abortion is performed for serious reasons, surveys of late abortion patients confirm that the vast majority occur because of delay in diagnosis of pregnancy. They are done for similar reasons as early abortions: relationship problems, young or old maternal age, education or financial concerns.

Late Abortions for Elective Reasons

Most of Tiller's abortions conformed to the generally elective character of these late-term procedures. Peggy Jarman of the Pro-Choice Action League stated that about three-fourths of Tiller's late-term patients were teenagers who denied to themselves or their families that they were pregnant until that fact could no longer be obscured. The Kansas Attorney General Phill Kline initiated a review of Tiller's records of late-term abortions. One of the nation's most distinguished psychiatrists, Dr. Paul R. McHugh, Johns Hopkins professor of psychiatry, was asked to determine if Tiller's patients satisfied Kansas requirement that they were likely to suffer a substantial and irreversible impairment if not allowed to abort. Dr. McHugh reviewed Tiller patient records and determined that they were not.

Although most late-term abortions are elective, it is claimed that serious maternal health problems require abortions. Intentional abortion for maternal health, particularly after viability, is one of the great deceptions used to justify all abortion. The very fact that the baby of an ill mother is viable raises the question of why, indeed, it is necessary to perform an abortion to end the pregnancy. With any serious maternal health problem, termination of pregnancy can be accomplished by inducing labor or performing a cesarean section, saving both mother and baby. If a mother needs radiation or chemotherapy for cancer, the mother's treatment can be postponed until viability, or regimens can be selected that will be better tolerated by the unborn baby. In modern neonatal intensive care units 90% of babies at 28 weeks survive, as do a significant percentage of those at earlier gestations.

Doctors Mislead About Necessity

T. Murphy Goodwin, M.D., a distinguished professor of maternal-fetal medicine at the University of Southern California, has written an eloquent article describing how women are told they need abortions for their own health, when this is patently untrue. A major reason for unnecessary abortion referrals is ignorance, to put it bluntly, especially on the part of physicians in medical specialties inexperienced in treating women with high-risk pregnancies. According to Goodwin, there are only three very rare conditions that result in a maternal mortality greater than 20% in the setting of late pregnancy. Even in these three situations there is room for latitude in waiting for fetal viability if the mother chooses to accept that risk.

Many women are ... not advised of all the possibilities for treatment and referred for abortion unnecessarily.

Goodwin's essay presents several cases in which pregnant women with cardiac conditions, cancer, or severe renal and autoimmune disease have been told categorically that they "needed" an abortion for their health or to save their life. But in every case the women were given wrong diagnoses, or incomplete information, and not offered any alternatives other than abortion. One example was a 38-year-old woman, 11 weeks pregnant, with breast cancer that had spread to the lymph nodes. She was told that chemotherapy offered her the best chance for survival, that she needed to abort her pregnancy prior to treatment, and that her prognosis was worse if she remained pregnant.

Liability Concerns

Goodwin states:

> We discussed with her published evidence that breast cancer is not affected by pregnancy and that the chemotherapy regimen required for her condition is apparently well-tolerated by the fetus. The experience with any given chemotherapy regimen is limited, and we were frank with the patient that there were open questions about long-term effects. When her physician was informed of the patient's desire to undergo chemotherapy and continue the pregnancy, he suggested that we take care of her and accept the liability. The patient underwent chemotherapy (Adriamycin and Cytoxan) and delivered a baby boy who appeared entirely normal at birth. That many chemotherapy regimens can be continued without apparent ill-effect in pregnancy is information readily available to any interested physician, but the patient was not informed.

In the prior case, the reluctance of the woman's physician to treat her was caused by a fear of being sued for unforeseen complications in the baby. An unfortunate reality is that the legal burden for the physician is severe if all possible risks of continuing the pregnancy are not communicated to the patient. In the U.S., multi-million dollar court judgments for "wrongful life" are allowed if the patients assert that they would have had an abortion had they known a particular problem might have ensued. It is impossible to foresee and enumerate each and every possible complication. But if abortion is recommended, even with minimal or no justification, there is no legal penalty. Many women are thus not advised of all the possibilities for treatment and referred for abortion unnecessarily. A good source of information to counter the pro-abortion bias among physicians in these difficult situations is consultation with a pro-life maternal fetal medicine specialist.

Fetal Deformities

Fetal problems are the other serious rationale for considering abortion, and diagnosis of these abnormalities has multiplied with the increased use of ultrasound in pregnancy. Ultrasound studies of fetal anatomy are often done at 18–20 weeks, so abortions done as a result of these scans are late abortions. But ultrasound is imperfect and analysis of the images can result in inaccurate interpretations. Pregnant women who have declined abortion for fetuses diagnosed by ultrasound with fatal birth defects such as Potter's syndrome (kidney disease with no amniotic fluid) or thanatophoric dwarfism (a fatal form of skeletal disease), have sometimes ended up giving birth to normal babies. Other parents have resisted recommended abortions for serious anatomical problems such as prune belly syndrome, omphalocele, congenital absence of the diaphragm, and other severe birth defects, and had their babies undergo surgical repair after birth. C. Everett Koop, M.D., the former surgeon general and renowned pediatric surgeon, was asked during the partial-birth abortion hearings if he had treated children "born with organs outside of their bodies" (omphalocele). Dr. Koop replied, "Oh, yes indeed. I've done that many times. The prognosis usually is good . . . the first child I ever did, with a huge omphalocele much bigger than her head, went on to develop well and become the head nurse in my intensive care unit many years later."

Perinatal Hospice as an Alternative

For fatal birth defects, abortion is sometimes presented as the only option. But a better alternative is perinatal hospice. This involves continuing the pregnancy until labor begins and giving birth normally, in a setting of comfort and support until natural death occurs. It is similar to what is done for families with terminally ill children and adults. Karen Santorum, a nurse and the wife of former Senator Rick Santorum, was faced with the prospect of her own son, Gabriel, being born with a fatal birth defect. She describes how Gabriel lived only two hours, but how in those two hours "we experienced a lifetime of emotions. Love, sorrow, regret, joy—all were packed into that brief span. To have rejected that experience would have been to reject life itself." The sense of peace and closure felt by families experiencing neonatal death in a hospice setting contrasts markedly with the experience of families undergoing abortion for fetal anomalies. Many couples who have had abortions for birth defects suffer from adverse long-term psychological effects and prolonged grief reactions. Children who learn that their mothers aborted their siblings can suffer feelings of worthlessness, guilt, distrust and rage.

Although parents choosing abortion may allege that the disabled child is better off not existing, disabled adults would contest that assertion.

Non-Fatal Defects

Non-fatal birth defects can be more challenging. The most common prenatal diagnosis resulting in mid-trimester abortion is Down syndrome. There has been an aggressive campaign by the American College of Obstetrics and Gynecology to use new technologies to detect Down syndrome in younger women through measurement of fetal neck-fold thickness and first trimester blood tests, now that prenatal diagnosis and abortion have succeeded in eliminating 90% of Down babies in women over 35. After diagnosis of Down syndrome, families are often not presented with an honest discussion of parenting their Down syndrome child, or the possibility of their Down syndrome child attending school and leading a semi-independent life. There are couples who are willing to adopt children with Down syndrome or other birth defects, but genetic counselors frequently do not give patients this information.

Diagnosis of a child with a fetal anomaly is life-changing and a major stress, but many families rise to the occasion and are able to cope with a disabled child. Although parents choosing abortion may allege that the disabled child is better off not existing, disabled adults would contest that assertion. When surveyed in numerous studies, no differences have been found between disabled and "able-bodied" people as to their satisfaction with life.

No Need for Late-Term Abortion

The Tiller murder, as well as the legislative and judicial hearings on partial-birth abortion, have exposed the public to a repugnant discussion of late-term abortion techniques, which include fetal dismemberment, partial-birth abortion, and feticidal injection of digoxin or potassium chloride into the unborn baby's heart preceding multi-day induction of labor. Late-term abortions result in more hemorrhage, lacerations and uterine perforations than early abortions, as well as risk of maternal death approaching that of carrying the baby to term. Subsequent pregnancies are at greater risk for loss or premature delivery due to trauma from late-term abortions. The psychological damage of aborting a late-term pregnancy, particularly one that is desired, can be profound and long lasting.

In conclusion, although serious threats to health can occur, there is always a life-affirming way to care for mother and baby, no matter how bleak the prognosis. The elimination of late-term abortion would not create a void in medical care, but would instead result in a more humane world in which vulnerable humans would be treated with the dignity and respect that they deserve.

CHAPTER 3

Is Abortion Harmful to Women and Society?

Chapter Preface

Abortion is often viewed as an individual choice that involves highly personal considerations and consequences, but it also plays a more public role in shaping population demographics and the character of society itself.

As authors in this chapter point out, due to a number of factors the African American community has an especially high rate of abortion, which alters the naturally occurring birth rate for that group. Another demographic group that is heavily influenced by abortion is women and girls—but this time on a global scale.

One hundred sixty million is roughly the number of girls and women alive in the United States today; it's also roughly the number of potential females who are *not* alive in Asia because prenatal sex identification via ultrasound and the wide availability of abortion have enabled women to avoid bearing girls in favor of having sons, which are culturally preferred in many societies.

Although the phenomenon isn't limited to Asia (lopsided birth ratios appear in the Balkans and Caucasus regions as well), China (with 121 boys per 100 girls), India (112:100) and Vietnam (111:100) show the most divergent numbers. The normal human birth ratio is 105 boys to 100 girls, a ratio that promotes population stability and social harmony.

While many observers decry the birth ratio phenomenon as "gendercide" against women and argue that gender discrimination lies at the heart of the disparity, rising global prosperity and the spread of Western attitudes and medical technologies are also contributing factors.

In her 2011 book, *Unnatural Selection: Choosing Boys over Girls, and the Consequences of a World Full of Men,* journalist Mara Hvistendahl points out that economic progress in developing countries means that more girls go to school and have access to better job opportunities when they grow up. As women become more socially and economically empowered, they also come to value having smaller families; their countries similarly value a declining birth rate as a sign of modernization. When urban, educated women do have children, they are more likely to be able to afford access to modern health care—including ultrasound exams that can determine the sex of a fetus and abortions to terminate unwanted pregnancies.

While many point to such trends as evidence of hard-won advances in women's self-determination and their increasing status worldwide, others note that the ultimate effect of that empowerment, at least in some countries, is skewed birth ratios due to sex-selective abortion.

"Because development is accompanied by plummeting birth rates," Hvistendahl writes, "it raises the stakes for each birth, increasing the chances parents will abort a female fetus. This triangle of concurrent trends—development, falling fertility, and sex selection—is alarming because it means sex selection won't simply disappear."[1]

Worldwide, thirty-six countries prohibit nonmedical sex selection and eight US states prohibit abortion motivated by the sex of the fetus. Public health officials say the extent of sex-selective abortion in the United States is hard to assess since it's rarely something women acknowledge, but it is believed to be of limited scope and primarily occurring within certain immigrant communities here.

There is growing concern, however, that the practice may become more widespread now that a simple new DNA blood test can determine a fetus's sex with 95 percent accuracy as early as seven weeks into pregnancy. Not only is the test reliable much sooner than an ultrasound, but it can be done in the privacy of one's own home, near the beginning of a preg-

1. Mara Hvistendahl, *Unnatural Selection: Choosing Boys over Girls, and the Consequences of a World Full of Men*, New York: PublicAffairs, 2011.

nancy. Then, if termination is desired, that can be done privately too; a medication abortion can be done at home before ten weeks of gestation—before most pregnancies even show.

"I think over the long run this [blood test] has the potential of changing attitudes toward pregnancy and to family," Audrey Chapman, a bioethicist at the University of Connecticut Health Center told *The New York Times*. "Women may be less invested in their pregnancies earlier than they are later, and the question has been raised whether women will look at their pregnancies increasingly as being conditional: 'I will keep this pregnancy only if.'"[2]

What impact the new blood test will have on women's decisions regarding abortion, both in the United States and as it becomes available globally, remains to be seen, but if previous sex-identifying technologies, such as ultrasounds, are any indicator, it won't be insignificant.

The authors in this chapter weigh abortion's relationship to racial discrimination, mental health, human rights, poverty, and public health as they consider the question of whether abortion is harmful to women and society.

2. Quoted in Pam Belluck, "If You Really, Really Wanted a Girl . . . ," *New York Times*, August 20, 2011. http://www.nytimes.com/2011/08/21/sunday-review/if-you-really -really-wanted-a-girl.html?_r=0.

Abortion Violates Human Rights

Ward Ricker

Pro-life activist Ward Ricker launched the Human Rights for All Ages campaign to draw attention to abortion as a grievous human rights violation.

Quiz for the day: Abortion is a

- religious issue

- social issue

- liberal or conservative issue

- human rights issue

If you chose any of the first three answers, I'm sorry, but you are wrong. Abortion is not a religious issue. It makes no difference what your religion is, or even whether you have any religion—abortion is wrong. Abortion is not a social issue. Somehow I do not think that if we had armed gangs roaming and shooting people dead in the middle of the streets that we would refer to this as a "social" issue. And dead preborn babies are no less dead and those killing them no less violent than people laying dead in the streets and their killers. Abortion is not a liberal or conservative issue. I don't care whether you consider yourself conservative, liberal, moderate, right-wing, left-wing, radical or however you wish to define yourself politically. Abortion is still wrong. Abortion is wrong because abortion kills little human beings. That makes it, purely and simply, a human rights issue, involving the most basic of all human rights, the right to life. It was no accident that the largest and most well known organization in the United States opposing abortion chose its name as "Right to Life". If we are not focused on human rights, we are not focused correctly.

We have allowed this dichotomy to develop between the concept of human rights and the concept of protecting the preborn and have not challenged it.

A Dichotomy of Human Rights Organizations

There is, however, a problem. In our world today there are numerous organizations that are looked up to and respected as being "human rights organizations". And, of course, these organizations unequivocally oppose the killing of preborn human beings, right? Wrong! About a year ago I did a survey of the organizations listed in the Yahoo directory as "human rights organizations" and found that out of more than 100 organizations, only three opposed abortion. Of the remaining 100-or-so organizations, approximately half actually advocated in favor of killing preborn human beings. Since creating the original list of human rights organizations, I have searched the Internet for other lists of such organizations. Out of the eleven such directories that I have found, how many times has Right to Life, American Life League, Feminists for Life, or any other of the well-known organizations or organizations that are listed in the Anti-Abortion Directory at AbortionReason .com that are fighting for the lives of our preborn children turned up on such lists? Once! (This recognition goes to Human Life International, listed in the Wikipedia listing. The three in the original list take a position in opposition to abortion, but it is "incidental" and not a primary focus of their work.)

In the eyes of the public, these organizations such as the ones in the Yahoo! Directory (groups like Amnesty International, Human Rights Watch, etc.) are the ones that stand for human rights. They stand for human rights, and yet they advocate in favor of abortion. What does this tell people? Another way to think of this is that there is a *dichotomy* in place separating the world of human rights advocacy and the world of anti-abortion advocacy. People see these as being two different things. They are not. It is we who stand up for the human rights of the preborn who are the true human rights advocates of our day. Organizations that support killing our youngest members are not human rights advocates, no matter what they may claim. This dichotomy can be clearly seen by a survey of today's media.

Highlighting Hypocrisy

The problem, however, is not so much that these organizations take such a stand, but rather that they get away with it. Why do they get away with it? Because we let them. Has there ever been a dedicated, sustained effort to confront these organizations and "call them on the carpet" for their stand in favor of killing people? Not that I am aware of. And this is the problem. How often do we have a presence at human rights events? I called around the the pro-life/anti-abortion organizations that are listed in the Anti-Abortion Directory to see what I could find out about the celebration of International Human Rights Day in their area. To my knowledge, after a great deal of research, there is only one organization that has represented the unborn at International Human Rights Day celebrations around the country. (Although there is one other organization that did make the attempt.)

Indeed, perhaps the majority of the people that I talked to in these groups had no idea what I was even talking about when I referred to the event. (Do you know when it is and what it commemorates?) Here are the groups fighting the greatest human rights violation on earth, and they have no knowledge of the one day set aside each year specifically for recognition of human rights! Are you seeing the problem here? We have allowed this dichotomy to develop between the concept of human rights and the concept of protecting the preborn and have not challenged it. In so doing we have become separated from what is recognized as human rights advocacy, and have allowed those who support killing to fill that role. Hence, when we try to speak out for the preborn, people think of us as a fringe group, or a special interest, or simply "those right-to-lifers".

Redefining the Anti-Abortion Movement

We will not succeed in ending abortion as long as people see us as religious zealots, or as a bunch of conservatives, or as those people who are trying to push our agenda. We will succeed when people see us as the true human rights advocates in the world today. We need to break the dichotomy that labels one group of organizations as "human rights" organizations, and delegates those groups that are fighting the greatest human rights tragedy of all to some other category. That is what the Human Rights for All Ages Campaign is all about. Yes, I wish to challenge these so-called "human rights" organizations to truly stand up for the human rights of all people. But we also need to refocus ourselves.

We need to be present at all human rights events and activities. . . . Indeed, we should not just be present, but we need to be leading the way; ours is, after all, the human rights cause of our day.

I wonder how many people chose one of the first three answers at the beginning of this article. I fear that often we ourselves have lost sight of the fact that we are fighting for the most basic of all human rights. Again, if we are not focused on human rights, we are not focused correctly. If we do not see ourselves and present ourselves as human rights advocates, people will not see us that way.

A New Campaign

The campaign addresses this problem in two ways. We contact the so-called "human rights" organizations and challenge them to actually stand up for human rights for *all* people—*all* ages. We need to put pressure on these groups and let them know that they cannot just blithely blunder forward and disregard the rights of a whole group of human beings. We must be alert to challenges by these groups or by others to try to subvert the rights of the preborn and raise our voices loudly when they do.

Even more importantly, though, we need to stand up and let people know that we are not separate from the human rights groups—we *are* the human rights groups. We cannot accept the dichotomy that has arisen. We must clear away the dichotomy in people's minds. But first we must clear away the dichotomy in our own minds and claim our place as the human rights advocates of today. This means that we need to be present at all human rights events and activities, such as International Human Rights Day, for example. Indeed, we should not just be present, but we need to be leading the way; ours is, after all, *the* human rights cause of our day.

A Human Rights Catastrophe

I am sure there are those out there who are asking, "Why should I take time from my important 'pro-life' work to bother with challenging pro-abortion groups and engaging in human-rights events?" I would hope by now that the answer is clear, but to clarify and summarize, ours is a human rights battle. However, the pro-abortion people have "claimed the high ground" in human rights, and human rights has come to be associated with "reproductive rights", "women's rights", "the right to choose", etc. As long as this remains the case, we will not succeed in convincing people of the worst human rights catastrophe that faces us today—the killing of preborn human beings. We need to first of all redirect our own thinking and remind ourselves that we are indeed fighting a human rights battle. We then need to stand up and challenge whenever any group or organization proposes killing in the name of human rights.

For Communities of Color,
Abortion Is Genocide

Abort73.com

Abort73.com is a website of Loxafamosity Ministries, a Christian nonprofit education corporation.

Abortion, by the numbers, is a racist institution. That's not to say that all or even most of those who support abortion are racists. Nor does it imply that there are not racists among those who oppose abortion. This statement has nothing to do with agendas or intent. It has everything to do with the simple, undeniable reality that in the United States, abortion kills minority children at more than three times the rate of non-Hispanic, white children. The Reverend Clenard H. Childress calls this phenomenon "black genocide," and has built a national ministry around its exposure.

Alveda C. King, daughter of slain civil-rights leader A.D. King and niece of Martin Luther King, Jr., quotes her uncle often when outlining her opposition of abortion. She writes: "[Martin Luther King, Jr.] once said, 'The Negro cannot win as long as he is willing to sacrifice the lives of his children for comfort and safety.' How can the 'Dream' survive if we murder the children? Every aborted baby is like a slave in the womb of his or her mother. The mother decides his or her fate."

A Look at the Numbers

Lest you feel these claims are an exaggeration, consider the numbers. According to 2010 census data, African Americans make up 12.6% of the U.S. population but the Centers for Disease Control (CDC) reports that black women accounted for 35.4% of all abortions in 2009. The Guttmacher Institute (AGI) puts the percentage of black abortions at 30% of the U.S. total. Their most recent numbers are from 2008. Similarly, AGI tells us that Hispanic women accounted for 25% of all U.S. abortions in 2008, though Hispanics make up just 16.3% of the U.S. population. The CDC lists the percentage of Hispanic abortions at 20.6%. Compare those numbers to non-Hispanic whites, who make up 63.7% of America's population, but account for only 36% of all U.S. abortions (37.7% according to the CDC).

> *To put it bluntly, abortion has thinned the black community in ways the Ku Klux Klan could have only dreamed of.*

Skewed Percentages

Every day in America, an average of 3,315 human beings lose their lives to abortion. Based on the percentages above, between 683–829 of those babies are Hispanic, between 1,193–1,174 are white, and between 995–1,207 are black. Not only are black children being killed at a far greater percentage than white children, it's possible they're being killed in greater numbers, period. Is that not shocking?! Though the white population in the U.S. outnumbers the black population five to one, abortion may well be killing more black children each day than white children. John Piper, a white pastor with a heart for racial justice, remarks on the disparity of abortion this way:

> The de facto effect (I don't call it the main cause, but net effect) of putting abortion clinics in the urban centers is that the abortion of Hispanic and Black babies is more than double their percentage of the population. Every day 1,300 black babies are killed in America. Seven hundred Hispanic babies die every day from abortion. Call this what you will—

when the slaughter has an ethnic face and the percentages are double that of the white community and the killers are almost all white, something is going on here that ought to make the lovers of racial equality and racial harmony wake up.

Abortion Spurs Demographic Shift

In 2009, a total of 286,623 blacks died in the U.S. That same year, an estimated 1.21 million abortions took place in the United States. If 35.4% were performed on black women, that means almost twice as many blacks were killed by abortion as by all other causes. In 2010, the black population in the U.S. stood just shy of 39 million. The CDC reports that during the 1970's, roughly 24% of all U.S. abortions were performed on black women. That percentage rose to 30% in the 1980's, 34% in the 1990's and 36% in the 2000's. That means that about 31% of all U.S. abortions since 1973 have been performed on African American women. Based on the January 2013 estimate that there have been 55.7 million abortions in the United States since 1973, we can deduce that approximately 17 million of the aborted babies were black.

No longer is [Planned Parenthood] driven by pregnancy prevention, it is now driven by pregnancy elimination.

Despite an overall black population growth of 12% between 2000 and 2010, the U.S. Census Bureau reports that the black population "grew at a slower rate than most other major race and ethnic groups in the country." CBS News reported in 2009 that "Hispanics have surpassed blacks as the nation's largest minority group." Can there be any question about the role abortion has played in this demographic shift? Despite similar population numbers, Hispanic women currently account for about 20% of all U.S. abortions, whereas African-American women account for 35%. From 1973 to 2012, abortion reduced the black population by 30%, and that doesn't even factor in all the children that would have been born to those aborted a generation ago. To put it bluntly, abortion has thinned the black community in ways the Ku Klux Klan could have only dreamed of.

Political Flip-Flops

The fact that black leaders, like President [Barack] Obama, support abortion rights does not change the reality of what is happening. How many candidates for public office have abandoned a prior conviction so as to be consistent with a party platform? This is perhaps nowhere more evident than in Reverend Jesse Jackson's flip-flop on abortion. Prior to having ambitions as a Presidential candidate for the Democratic Party, he was an incredibly eloquent and outspoken opponent of abortion. Though his public stance on abortion has reversed, his earlier remarks remain as applicable as ever, and show that there is more than mere numbers at stake. Abortion attacks the "moral fabric" of an entire people. The following remarks come from his 1977 article for the *National Right to Life News*:

> The question of "life" is The Question of the 20th century. Race and poverty are dimensions of the life question, but discussions about abortion have brought the issue into focus in a much sharper way.

> How we will respect and understand the nature of life itself is the over-riding moral issue, not of the Black race, but of the human race.

> The question of abortion confronts me in several different ways. First, although I do not profess to be a biologist, I have studied biology and know something about life from the point of view of the natural sciences. Second, I am a minister of the Gospel and, therefore, feel that abortion has a religious and moral dimension that I must consider. Third,

I was born out of wedlock (and against the advice that my mother received from her doctor) and therefore abortion is a personal issue for me.

From my perspective, human life is the highest good, the summum bonum. Human life itself is the highest human good and God is the supreme good because He is the giver of life. . . .

There are those who argue that the right to privacy is of higher order than the right to life. I do not share that view. I believe that life is not private, but rather it is public and universal.

If one accepts the position that life is private, and therefore you have the right to do with it as you please, one must also accept the conclusion of that logic. That was the premise of slavery. You could not protest the existence or treatment of slaves on the plantation because that was private and therefore outside of your right to be concerned.

Another area that concerns me greatly, namely because I know how it has been used with regard to race, is the psycholinguistics involved in this whole issue of abortion. If something can be dehumanized through the rhetoric used to describe it, then the major battle has been won. Those advocates of taking life prior to birth do not call it killing or murder, they call it abortion. They further never talk about aborting a baby because that would imply something human. Rather they talk about aborting the fetus. Fetus sounds less than human and therefore can be justified.

. . . What happens to the mind of a person, and the moral fabric of a nation, that accepts the aborting of the life of a baby without a pang of conscience? What kind of a person, and what kind of a society will we have 20 years hence if life can be taken so casually?

It is that question, the question of our attitude, our value system, and our mind-set with regard to the nature and worth of life itself that is the central question confronting mankind. Failure to answer that question affirmatively may leave us with a hell right here on earth.

Planned Parenthood's Purpose

The majority of Planned Parenthood's abortion clinics are located in communities with minority populations that exceed the city or state averages. Is this a bizarre coincidence, or is it merely an extension of the eugenic principles that seem to have driven Planned Parenthood's founder, Margaret Sanger, a founder who is documented as saying, "We do not want the word to go out that we want to exterminate the Negro population." This statement, written in a 1939 letter to a colleague, can be taken in one of two ways. Either she didn't want the black community to *wrongly* assume that her efforts promoting birth control were an attempt to eliminate them, *or* she didn't want the black community to find out that this is exactly what she had in mind. Planned Parenthood assumes the first; her opponents assume the latter. Based on the greater context of her writings, the truth likely lies in between. She probably didn't have in mind the elimination of all blacks, but it is quite reasonable to infer that she did want to keep them in submission and in line.

Whatever the case may be, the bottom line is this. Margaret Sanger's vision of social purification was rooted in birth control and sterilization. Compared with abortion, these were minor threats to minority communities. Planned Parenthood's contemporary vision of social purification is much more menacing. No longer is the organization driven by pregnancy prevention, it is now driven by pregnancy elimination. We can debate the racial intent of Planned Parenthood past and present, but we cannot debate the results. Abortion is by no means an equal opportunity killer.

Safe and Legal Abortion Benefits Public Health

Jodi Jacobson

Jodi Jacobson is the editor-in-chief of RH Reality Check, *a daily online publication that provides news, analysis, and commentary on sexual and reproductive health and justice issues.*

During a hearing that ranged from questions on judicial temperment and private property to the role of precedent in court decisions and [then-prospective Supreme Court Justice Sonia] Sotomayor's decision on the use of nunchucks, the most direct, probing, and potentially telling questions came from Senator Lindsay Graham (R-South Carolina).

Among the questions Graham posed to Sotomayor: "Is abortion a public health issue?"

Maybe it was my impression, but Sotomayor seemed to pause carefully before answering this question.

My answer: Unequivocally yes. When women lack access to safe abortion services, they die . . . as they did historically in the United States and as is the case in countries throughout the world today. Moreover, high rates of maternal mortality are related to high rates of infant and child mortality. Complications of unsafe abortion are among the leading causes of maternal death in many countries, and in some, like Peru, unsafe abortion is the single most important cause of maternal illness and death. This is a critical public health issue.

The question was put to Judge Sotomayor by Senator Graham in a clear effort to pin her down on her positions regarding choice. Graham—with whom I disagree deeply on many issues but for whom I have considerable respect in no small part because I perceive him as less likely to grandstand for the sake of it and who often speaks very frankly—asked Soto-mayor a number of questions about her relationship to the Puerto Rican Legal Defense and Education Fund (PRLDEF) with which the nominee was associated for 12 years, in part as a board member.

A Public Health Issue

Because of that association, I have to believe that Judge Soto-mayor understands the public health dimensions of access to safe abortion services. PRLDEF advocated for Medicaid funding of abortion for low-income women, recognizing that the lack of access among women to abortion services resulting from lack of the means to pay represented a public health as well as a human rights issue. According to [the Associated Press], for example:

> The 1980 Supreme Court case, *Williams v. David Zbaraz*, challenged an Illinois law that said state money could not be used to pay for abortions for poor people, except when necessary to save the life of the mother.
>
> The Puerto Rican Legal Defense and Education Fund board, along with three other organizations, filed an amicus brief with the Supreme Court, arguing that banning taxpayer-funded abortions discriminated against poor minority women. At the time, Sotomayor served on the group's board of directors.

Different groups within society face different conditions legally, economically and socially and therefore have different experiences than the average white male Senator or male Supreme Court Justice.

In fact, this is a critical social justice and public health issue for low-income and minority women who do not have access either to preventive reproductive health services or other forms of preventive care.

141

(PRLDEF also litigated employment discrimination and related cases probed by Republicans.)

Response Raises Concerns

But Judge Sotomayor did not address the question, responding instead that any advocate speaks on behalf of the interests of their client, as the client determines them based on their own needs and experiences and their reading of the law. PRLDEF, she stated, represented its clients—the women involved and their needs. These needs were defined and arose from their own immediate and historical experiences. Their experiences shaped their position legally and otherwise.

And this, perhaps, is at least part of the reason why there is such a great degree of anxiety on the part of the far right about the so-called wise Latina quote. As I wrote in my previous post on the hearings, that quote has been taken out of context by many Senators as well as by the mainstream media, which has largely failed to correct the storyline created by the far right message machine. But it is a fact that in a country where race, ethnicity and income still play a huge role in access to resources including basic health care, employment and in other areas, where health disparities remain great, and where institutionalized racism still exists, different individuals and different groups within society face different conditions legally, economically and socially and therefore have different experiences than the average white male Senator or male Supreme Court Justice.

Knowing that Sotomayor can identify with these needs and appears to deeply understand both those facts as well as her need to be an impartial and effective judge appears to drive the far right over the edge.

Saying Much by Saying Little

Moreover, given she was involved with the PRLDEF, it is unimaginable that Sotomayor is not knowledgeable about, for example, the reproductive rights violations—from lack of access to basic care to forced sterilizations—that mar the histories and shape the experiences of women of Puerto Rican descent in the same way as they do women of other minority groups.

Graham also asked whether abortion was a civil rights issue. And as she did with the public health question, Sotomayor deflected the question.

I know that Graham was looking for a way to pin her down on her views about choice in ways that could be used and abused in the media to her detriment and to the detriment of women everywhere. She stood firm and kept control of the conversation. And while it was only a part of a daylong hearing, for me this was one of the most telling exchanges, because while Sotomayor did not affirm the role of access to safe abortion services in public health, nor its human rights implications for women she also refused to deny it. And women need another (and after her yet another) Supreme Court justice who understands that data, experience, empathy and real life do matter and are part of the weaving of the fabric of our laws in profound ways, even when we are unwilling to admit this.

Groundbreaking New Study: What Happens to Women Who Can't Get Abortions

Kathleen Geier

Kathleen Geier is a writer and public policy researcher who lives in Chicago. She blogs at Inequality Matters.

Abortion is one of the most common surgical procedures in the United States, and one of the central political issues of our time. Yet in spite of this, there is surprisingly little solid social science research on many of the important social, psychological, and economic consequences of abortion outcomes. Having good research on abortion is important, because research findings are often used to justify abortion policy and law.

For example, in the Supreme Court's 2007 *Carhart* case, which upheld a ban on so-called "partial birth abortion," Justice Anthony Kennedy's decision infamously invoked the paternalistic notion that protecting women from possible negative consequences of their own decision to abort justified abortion restrictions. In the *Carhart* opinion, Kennedy was influenced by junk social science studies by anti-abortion advocates claiming that women who have abortions suffer from a "post-abortion syndrome" characterized by regret and severe mental health issues. There is no scientific evidence that post-abortion syndrome exists, but that didn't stop Kennedy from basing his decision on its alleged effects anyway.

One extremely important question Kennedy didn't give much thought to is the other side of the question: that is, what happens to women who seek abortions but are denied them. For reasons of both ideology and feasibility, this issue had not been studied much—until now, that is. Researchers at the University of California in San Francisco are currently conducting a major longitudinal study of just this question. Known as the Turnaway Study, this project is examining "the mental health, physical health and socioeconomic outcomes of receiving an abortion compared to carrying an unwanted pregnancy to term." The findings thus far suggest that women who are denied abortions fare significantly less well than those who are able to obtain them.

I'll discuss those findings later, but first I wanted to describe the study's methodology. Working with first and second trimester abortion clinics, researchers recruited about 1,000 participants who fell into these three groups:

> women whose gestational age was one day to three weeks over the gestational limit and who were turned away from the clinic without receiving an abortion; women whose gestational age was one day to two weeks under the clinic's gestational limit and who received an abortion; and women who received a medical or surgical abortion in the first trimester of pregnancy.

Anti-abortion advocates often claim that women who abort are more likely to develop drug problems. However, the study suggests that that is not the case; abortion did not increase the risk of drug use.

The women were interviewed by phone every six months, for a period of five years. They were questioned about subjects including their physical and mental health, educational attainment, financial and employment status, family life, and, for women who carried their pregnancies to term, their parenting issues and children's well-being. The researchers have recently begun to release the preliminary findings, which have not yet been published. They presented them at a recent meeting of the American Public Health Association. Here are some of the highlights:

- Most women (86%) who carried their pregnancy to term kept their baby; 11% gave the baby up for adoption.

- Being denied an abortion appears to have impoverished women and had a negative effect on their employment status. Researchers say that at the beginning of the study, there weren't any economic differences between those who got an abortion and those who were denied one.

However, after a year, "[W]omen denied abortion were more likely to be receiving public assistance (76% vs. 44%) and have household income below the FPL [Federal Poverty Level] (67% vs. 56%) than women who received an abortion. The proportion of women denied an abortion who were working full time was lower than among women who received an abortion (48% vs. 58%)."

- Anti-abortion advocates often claim that women who abort are more likely to develop drug problems. However, the study suggests that that is not the case; abortion did not increase the risk of drug use.

- One year later, those denied an abortion were significantly more likely to have experienced domestic violence in the past six months and significantly less likely to rate their relationship with their child's father as good or very good. At the study's baseline, there were no differences in these areas between the two groups.

Some cautionary notes about these findings: first, they are not the final results. Second, they have not yet been published in a peer-reviewed journal, so it's possible they may not past muster scientifically.

Third, as is the case with every social science study, it is not necessarily clear whether the outcomes are the result of causation or correlation. The study's methodology appears to be sound; the sample size is large, and according to researchers, there were no notable observed differences between the control group (those who got an abortion) vs. the experimental group (those who didn't). Nevertheless, there is reason to wonder whether there were in fact significant *un*observed differences between the two groups. Women who are unable to organize themselves to get an abortion before it's too late may be suffering from more financial or emotional problems than those who get one in time.

The women who were denied abortions fared significantly less well on virtually all fronts.

It's also possible that they may feel more ambivalent about their decision to abort in the first place. If any of these differences exist at the outset, then the worse outcomes for the women who were denied abortion could be due to those pre-existing factors, and not the denial of abortion in and of itself. There are statistical techniques that researchers can use to control for observed and unobserved differences, but in the end separating correlation from causation is always a thorny issue. You can never know what would have happened to the turned away women in a counterfactual universe where they were able to get the abortions they needed.

Those caveats aside, the study may well prove to be the largest and best study of its kind we get, and its findings appear to be valid and reliable. In that light, the results are illuminating, and alarming. The women who were denied abortions fared significantly less well on virtually all fronts. One of the most basic and most powerful tenets of feminism is that, contra Justice Kennedy's insulting paternalism, women themselves are the best judge of what is good for them. These study findings strongly support that conclusion; women who received abortions did much better than those who were denied abortions against their will. This suggests that if the women had received the abortions they sought, they would have fared better as well. Trusting women is not only common sense, it makes excellent public policy sense as well.

Abortion Does Not Increase Mental Health Problems for Women

Denis Campbell

Denis Campbell is a health correspondent for The Guradian, *a daily newspaper in the United Kingdom.*

Having an abortion does not increase a woman's chance of developing mental health problems, according to a large study that challenges anti-abortion groups' claims that termination causes trauma and depression.

The research, commissioned by the Academy of Medical Royal Colleges and funded by the Department of Health [in the United Kingdom], should reassure women that they are at no greater risk than if they give birth, the authors said.

The biggest study worldwide of the relationship between termination and mental wellbeing is published and concludes: "The best current evidence suggests that it makes no difference to a woman's mental health whether she chooses to have an abortion or to continue with the pregnancy."

The research undertaken by the National Collaborating Centre for Mental Health (NCCMH) at the Royal College of Psychiatrists assessed 44 studies from 1990-2011 which examined data on hundreds of thousands of women at least 90 days after an abortion.

The researchers found that an unwanted pregnancy does involve a heightened risk of mental health problems, but added that the rates were no different whether they had an abortion or give birth.

Professor Tim Kendall, director of the NCCMH, said that about a third of women who have an unwanted pregnancy suffered depression and anxiety compared to 11% to 12% of the general population.

An unwanted pregnancy may cause mental health problems, a woman may already have problems before becoming pregnant, or it could be a combination of the two, he added.

Helping Women Cope

The review had looked at only the mental health aspects of abortion, not the ethics of abortion or its physical consequences, Kendall added. Research should now concentrate on helping women cope with the impact of an unwanted pregnancy.

Women with a history of mental problems were more likely to experience problems after a termination, and other factors such as being pressured by a partner to have a termination could also increase the chance, the researchers found.

Tracey McNeill, the vice-president of Marie Stopes, which performs 66,000 abortions a year in Britain, said the review reinforced its belief that having an abortion has no greater effect on a woman's mental health than continuing with a pregnancy.

What is clear is that having an unwanted pregnancy has implications for people's mental health and wellbeing.

She said: "In our experience, for every extra week a woman carries an unwanted pregnancy, it can represent an extra week of distress. This is reinforced by the review's finding that while abortion does not have a disproportionate impact on mental health, having an unwanted pregnancy does.

"This coincides with our strong belief that all women should be able to access non-directive counselling, then be able to exercise their right to be referred for an abortion without delay, if this is the option they have chosen."

Dr Kate Guthrie of the Royal College of Obstetricians and Gynaecologists said it had revised its guidelines to take account of these findings. "The recommendations highlight the need for service providers to inform women about the range of emotional responses that may be experienced during and following an abortion."

Anne Milton, the public health minister, said the findings of "this important review" would be considered when the Department of Health updates its sexual health strategy next year. "What is clear is that having an unwanted pregnancy has implications for people's mental health and wellbeing", she added.

Findings Refuted

Anthony Ozimic, of the anti-abortion Society for the Protection of Unborn Children, dismissed the study's findings as predictable, accused its authors of ignoring key studies and said evidence showed that abortion involved an increased risk of depression and post-traumatic stress.

"Clinical case studies and stories written and told by many women confirm empirical findings of the psychological harms of abortion," he said.

"Prior mental health may influence mental health after abortion, but does not begin to account for all of the effect. Abortion is associated with severe negative psychological complications for some women.

"Women experienced feelings such as shame, guilt, grief and regret after an abortion."

CHAPTER 4

Should Access to
Abortion Be Restricted?

Overview: Access to Abortion Varies Widely from State to State

Alina Salganicoff, Adara Beamesderfer, and Nisha Kurani

Alina Salganicoff is vice president and director of women's health policy at the Henry J. Kaiser Family Foundation, a nonprofit research organization that focuses on national health-care issues and global health policy. Adara Beamesderfer is a policy associate and Nisha Kurani is a program associate for the Foundation's women's health policy team.

The Patient Protection and Affordable Care Act (ACA) makes significant changes to health coverage for women by expanding access to coverage and broadening the health benefits that many will receive. In January 2014 the coverage expansions to assist uninsured individuals gain access to coverage took effect. The issue of abortion coverage was at the heart of many debates in the run up to the passage of the law and continues to the present day. This brief summarizes the major coverage provisions of the ACA that are relevant for women of reproductive age, reviews current federal and state policies on Medicaid [the state and federal government's health insurance program for the poor] and insurance coverage of abortion services, and presents national and state estimates on the availability of abortion coverage for women who are newly eligible for Medicaid or private coverage as a result of the ACA.

Signed into law on March 23, 2010, the ACA is a federal law that aims to ensure that U.S. citizens and legal residents have health insurance by requiring most individuals to obtain

Adapted by the Editor, based on "Coverage for Abortion Services and the ACA," The Henry J. Kaiser Family Foundation, September 2014. Copyright © 2014 by the Henry J. Kaiser Family Foundation. All rights reserved. Reproduced by permission.

a minimum level of insurance coverage. This is to be achieved through a combination of public and private insurance expansions. The ACA was designed to expand health care coverage to the poorest uninsured by extending Medicaid eligibility to all qualifying individuals with incomes up to 138% of the federal poverty level (FPL). The 2012 Supreme Court ruling, however, had the effect of giving states the option to expand their Medicaid programs rather than requiring this expansion, as was the design of the ACA. As of January 2014, 25 states and the District of Columbia have expanded Medicaid eligibility, but 25 states have not, leaving millions of poor individuals without a pathway to affordable coverage.

The federal Hyde Amendment restricts state Medicaid programs from using federal funds to cover abortions beyond the cases of life endangerment, rape, or incest.

The ACA also includes reforms that aim to make insurance more affordable and accessible. Individuals with incomes above the federal poverty level will be able to obtain insurance through healthcare Marketplaces, also known as exchanges, which will offer a variety of plans from which they can purchase insurance. To help those with low and moderate incomes with the costs of insurance, the federal government will provide subsidies (in the form of premium tax credits) to eligible individuals and families with incomes between 100% and 400% FPL. All of the plans offered on the Marketplace must provide coverage for 10 Essential Health Benefits (EHB). Abortion services, however, are explicitly excluded from the list of EHBs that all plans are required to offer.

Federal and State Laws Regarding Abortion

Since 1977, federal law has banned the use of any federal funds for abortion, unless the pregnancy is a result of rape, incest, or if it is determined to endanger the woman's life.

This rule, also known as the Hyde Amendment, is not a permanent law; rather it has been attached annually to Congressional appropriations bills, and has been approved every year by the Congress. The Hyde Amendment initially affected only funding for abortions under Medicaid, but over the years, its reach broadened to limit federal funds for abortion for federal employees and women in the Indian Health Service. Until recently, insurance coverage of abortion for women in the military had been even more restricted so that pregnancies resulting from rape or incest were not covered. In early 2013, an amendment to the National Defense Authorization Act expanded insurance coverage to include abortions of pregnancies resulting from rape or incest. There is still a ban on federal funds to pay for abortions in other circumstances and abortions still cannot be provided at any military treatment facility except in cases of life endangerment, rape or incest.

Medicaid Restrictions

State level policies also have a large impact on how insurance and Medicaid cover abortions, particularly since states are responsible for operation of Medicaid programs and insurance regulation. The Medicaid program serves millions of low-income women and is a major funder of reproductive health services nationally. Approximately two-thirds of adult women on Medicaid are in their reproductive years. As discussed earlier, the federal Hyde Amendment restricts state Medicaid programs from using federal funds to cover abortions beyond the cases of life endangerment, rape, or incest. However, if a state chooses to, it can use its own funds to cover abortions in other circumstances. Currently, 17 states use state-only funds to pay for abortions for women on Medicaid in circumstances different than those federal limitations set in the Hyde Amendment. In 32 states and the District of Columbia, Medicaid programs do not pay for any abortions beyond the Hyde exceptions.

The ACA reinforces the current Hyde Amendment restrictions, continuing to limit federal funds to pay only for abortions to terminate pregnancies that endanger the life of the woman or that are a result of rape or incest. State Medicaid programs continue to have the option to cover abortions in other circumstances using only state funds and no federal funds. President [Barack] Obama issued an executive order as part of health reform that restated the federal limits specifically for Medicaid coverage of abortion. The law also explicitly does not preempt other current state policies regarding abortion, such as parental consent or notification, waiting period laws or any of the abortion limits or coverage requirements that states have enacted.

In states that do not bar coverage of abortions on plans available through the Marketplace, insurers may offer a plan that covers abortions beyond the federal limitations, but this coverage must be paid for using private, not federal, dollars.

The Private Sector

In the private insurance sector, where states have the authority to regulate plans that are issued in the state, 9 states impose restrictions on the circumstances under which insurance will cover abortions in Medicaid, Marketplace plans, and private insurance. Some states follow the same restrictions as the federal Hyde Amendment for their private plans, while some are more restrictive. Oklahoma has exceptions for cases of rape, incest involving a minor, or to save the woman's life. Utah has exceptions to save the life of the mother or avert serious risk of loss of a major bodily function, if the fetus has a defect as documented by a physician that is uniformly diagnosable and lethal, and in cases of rape or incest. However, six states (Idaho, Kansas, Kentucky, Missouri, Nebraska, and North

Dakota) have an exception only to save the woman's life. Michigan only allows abortion coverage when the abortion increases the probability of a live birth, preserves the life or health of the child after live birth, or to remove a fetus that has died as a result of natural causes, accidental trauma, or a criminal assault on the pregnant woman. Five states had these laws on the books prior to the ACA, and four more states have passed new laws banning private plan coverage post-ACA. While eight of these states allow insurers to sell riders for abortion coverage on the private market, there is little evidence about their availability and no documentation of their cost or impact on access. Utah does not allow riders to be sold for abortion coverage.

States Set the Rules

Because the ACA explicitly prohibits states from including abortion in any essential benefits package, states or insurers offering plans in a state Marketplace will not be required to offer abortion coverage. The ACA also stipulates that each state Marketplace must include at least one plan that does not cover abortions beyond those permitted by current federal law. States can also pass laws that bar all plans participating in the state Marketplace from covering abortions, which 24 states have done since the ACA was signed into law in 2010. Most states include narrow exceptions for women whose pregnancies endanger their life or are the result of rape or incest, but two states (Louisiana and Tennessee) do not provide for any exceptions. The ACA prohibits plans in the state Marketplaces from discriminating against any provider because of "unwillingness" to provide abortions.

In states that do not bar coverage of abortions on plans available through the Marketplace, insurers may offer a plan that covers abortions beyond the federal limitations, but this coverage must be paid for using private, not federal, dollars. Plans must notify consumers of the abortion coverage as part of the summary of benefits and coverage explanation at the time of enrollment. The ACA outlines a methodology for states to follow to ensure that no federal funds are used towards coverage for abortions beyond the Hyde limitations. Any plan that covers abortions beyond Hyde limitations must estimate the actuarial value of such coverage by taking into account the cost of the abortion benefit (valued at least $1 per enrollee per month). This estimate cannot take into account any savings that might be achieved as a result of the abortions (such as prenatal care or delivery).

Separate Funding Sources

Furthermore, the federal rules stipulate that plans that offer abortion coverage and receive federal subsidies (it is believed that all plans in the state Marketplace will receive at least some federal subsidies) need to collect two premium payments, so that the funds go into separate accounts. One payment would be for the value of the abortion benefit and the other payment would be for the value of all other services. The funds are to be deposited in separate allocation accounts, overseen for compliance by state health insurance commissioners. Multi-state health insurance plans offered through state Marketplaces are prohibited from offering abortion coverage beyond Hyde Amendment restrictions so that individuals in all states will have a choice of enrolling in a plan that does not cover abortion if they so choose.

Women and Health Coverage

There are 11.8 million uninsured women of reproductive age (ages 19 to 49) legally residing in the United States. Of these uninsured women, an estimated 3.4 million (29%) now qualify for Medicaid or have been eligible, but had not previously enrolled in the program. About 4.8 million women (40%) have incomes between 100–400% of the Federal Poverty Level (FPL) and now qualify for subsidies in the form of tax credits if they obtain coverage through their state Marketplace. There are about 1.8 million uninsured women with incomes at or above 400% of FPL who can now obtain coverage on the state Marketplace or through the individual market, but do not qualify for subsidies because their income is too high. Finally, an estimated 1.8 million uninsured women fall into the so-called "coverage gap" because they live in one of the 25 states that is not expanding Medicaid and their income is below 100% FPL, leaving them ineligible for subsidies to purchase coverage on the health care Marketplace under the law.

Women who seek an abortion but do not have coverage for the service will need to shoulder the out-of-pocket costs of the services.

Coverage Gap States

Because of the Hyde Amendment rules and the state laws that govern coverage of abortion services in private plans, the availability of abortion coverage is uneven across the states among the women who are newly eligible for Medicaid and private coverage. Of the estimated 11.8 million women who are uninsured and legally present in the United States, about half (52%) will be able to enroll in a Medicaid plan or private insurance plan that does not limit the scope of coverage for abortion services if they wish. One third, 3.9 million women, live in a state where they can only enroll in a private or Medicaid plan that limits abortion coverage either to pregnancy that results from rape or incest or a medical threat to a woman's life as in the Hyde Amendment or in some states even more limited circumstances. About 1.8 million women (15%) are in the coverage gap and do not have access to affordable coverage, either to Medicaid or subsidies, because their state did not expand Medicaid and their incomes are too low to qualify for tax credits under the law. Twenty-three of the twenty-five states that are not expanding Medicaid are states that follow the Hyde Amendment. Two states, Montana and Alaska, use state-only funds to cover abortions beyond the Hyde limits but are not expanding Medicaid eligibility. As a result, nearly all of the women in the coverage gap states (99%) would still have restricted availability of abortion coverage under Medicaid even if their state were to broaden eligibility.

Limited Availability

The availability of abortion coverage varies considerably by state due to differences in state policies that limit abortion in Medicaid, on state Marketplaces, and/or in the private sector. In 9 states, uninsured women will only be able to obtain coverage in Medicaid or private plans that place limits on the circumstances in which they can use the insurance to pay for the abortion or will not gain coverage because their state is not expanding Medicaid. This is because the state in which they reside has passed laws that limit coverage in both private plans and those available on the Marketplace and, in the case of those that are expanding Medicaid, also do not use state dollars to pay for abortions in their Medicaid programs beyond Hyde rules, or are not expanding Medicaid. In contrast, in 14 states, uninsured women who will be newly eligible for Medicaid, tax credits, or unsubsidized coverage will all have the option of enrolling in a plan that offers coverage for abortion without limitations.

Women who seek an abortion but do not have coverage for the service will need to shoulder the out-of-pocket costs of the services. The cost of an abortion varies depending on factors such as location, facility, timing, and type of procedure. A clinic-based abortion at 10 weeks' gestation is estimated to cost between $400 and $550, whereas an abortion at 20-21 weeks' gestation is estimated to cost $1,100-$1,650 or more. Though the vast majority (~90%) of abortions are performed early in pregnancy, the costs could still be economically challenging for many low-income women. Approximately 5% of abortions are performed at 16 weeks or later in the pregnancy. For women with medically-complicated health situations or who need a second-trimester abortion, the costs could be prohibitive. In some cases, women may have to delay their abortion while they have time to raise funds, or women may only learn of a fetal anomaly in the second trimester when the costs are considerably higher.

The impact of the abortion coverage restrictions will be disproportionately felt by poor and low-income women who have limited ability to pay for abortion services with out-of-pocket funds.

Abortion Faces Broader Challenges

While millions of women stand to gain health insurance coverage as a result of the ACA insurance expansions, many will have insurance plans that restrict the circumstances in which abortion services will be covered. As a result of state actions to limit coverage of abortion in the Marketplace plans and federal law limiting abortion coverage under Medicaid, one third of women newly eligible for coverage can only enroll in a plan that restricts abortion coverage to limited circumstances. About half of women of reproductive age who are legally residing in the U.S. qualify for coverage in plans that do not have limitations, and 15% are in the coverage gap and will not qualify for Medicaid or affordable coverage.

These coverage limitations are occurring at a time when many states are taking other actions to curtail access to abortion through multiple fronts. These efforts include state level legislation that focuses on the doctors and clinics that provide abortion services to women. Some state legislatures are enacting laws that expand the regulatory requirements on abortion clinics, place gestational limits on when women can have abortions, include new rules for women to have ultrasounds and multiple visits, and impose new regulations on clinicians such as requiring them to have hospital admitting privileges. In addition, legislative activity has focused on prohibiting certain providers and clinics that perform abortions from qualifying for any public financing, including Title X allotments and Medicaid funds, even when those funds are specifically required to be used for other services such as family planning and other preventive services and not abortions.

Low-Income Women Feel Impact Most

The impact of the abortion coverage restrictions will be disproportionately felt by poor and low-income women who have limited ability to pay for abortion services with out-of-pocket funds. The effect of the absence of abortion coverage could be magnified by laws that have been enacted in some states requiring that additional services, such as sonograms, be performed before all abortions or by the multiple visits and waiting periods that are required in some states which will result in increased costs of abortion procedures and higher travel costs. These requirements, along with policies that increase the regulations on clinics and providers, will have the expected result of limiting access to and the availability of abortion services in some states.

At the federal level, further efforts to limit abortion coverage have recently focused on legislation that would ban the availability of federal tax credits to individuals who purchase Marketplace health plans that include coverage of abortions. This bill, HR7, would also limit tax credits to small businesses that offer plans that include abortion coverage to their employees. In the coming years as the ACA is implemented, the laws that are enacted at the federal and state levels as well as the choices that are made by insurers, employers, and policy holders will ultimately determine the extent of abortion coverage that will be available to women across the nation.

Abortion Should Be Banned, Regardless of the Circumstances

Patrick Johnston

Patrick Johnston is director of the Association of Pro-Life Physicians, a professional organization for physicians who oppose abortion.

The Sixth Commandment states, "You shall not murder."

It's a commandment that even mass murderers keep most of the time. They just make an exception every now and then. The devil doesn't want to overthrow God's law—he just wants you to make an exception. Our exceptions to God's commandments, however, are indeed a challenge to God's authority and an assault against His Word-law. If you make an exception to the commandment "Thou shalt not murder" then in that instance, you have violated it. All sophistry aside, there are no exceptions to the divine ordinance against intentionally killing innocent people, and to fancy exceptions is to usurp God's rule and set up a counterfeit moral standard after Lucifer's example.

A Pro-Life Rebellion Is Afoot

There is a pro-life rebellion afoot that is distinguishing itself from the mainstream pro-life movement and is indicting it for complicity in the Abortion Holocaust. Personhood Amendments are a perfect example; through amending state constitutions to define person to include unborn children, states are trying to end all abortion without exception within their borders. As of August 2014, 1.4 million people have signed a Personhood petition in state ballot initiatives, and thrice states have brought their Personhood Amendment to the ballot box on an Election Day. Many Personhood leaders do not believe that the goal of their Amendment is to overturn *Roe v. Wade*; on the contrary, they believe *Roe v. Wade* is unlawful, invalid, and ultimately inconsequential to their duty to protect every child within their lawful jurisdiction. Predictably, one of the greatest threats to these attempts to protect every child statewide by love and by law are "pro-life" groups and "pro-life" leaders who favor exceptions or who believe states have a duty to submit to lawless and unconstitutional judicial tyranny. Regardless, these signature-gathering personhood warriors are akin to the "slavery abolitionists" of the civil war era, standing on principle and on God's Word, and exposing all wet-finger-raising compromisers as accomplices in the Abortion Holocaust.

From Pragmatism to Principle

Another example of this pro-life shift from pragmatism to principle is found in a movement of Hippocratic physicians that began in 2004 in Muskingum County, Ohio. In that county, fifteen physicians from a dozen different specialties have publicly stated that they are convinced that life begins at fertilization, and have committed not to do abortions nor refer for abortions. Billboards have erupted that claim, over the backdrop of a ten-week old human *fetus*, "Does your doctor kill babies? www.ProLifePhysicians.org." Physicians are joining this group—the Association of Pro-Life Physicians—from all over the country, longing to be distinguished from colleagues that are, unfortunately, willing to kill their patients. The most controversial element of this crusade to draw a line in the sand over the issue of abortion is that doctors who are "pro-life with exceptions" are being left on the side with the unabashed abortionists. Whether you kill thirty people a day for a living, or whether you are simply an accomplice in one murder of one child conceived through rape or incest, you are a murderer. God's Word makes it plain: "He that keepeth the whole law, and offends in one point, is guilty of all" (James 2:10). Indeed, our exceptions define our principles and reveal our heart.

We should never abandon our principles in our response to [the] difficult, heart-wrenching scenarios.

It makes perfect sense for politicians to make pragmatic exceptions to the pro-life ethic, especially if they are running against an openly pro-choice opponent. When George W. Bush, John McCain, and Mitt Romney ran for President, they publicly justified abortion in some cases, and had funded Planned Parenthood in previous positions of leadership, with no promise to cease doing so. In spite of this, they gained the endorsement of National Right to Life and almost every pro-life organization in the country. Pro-lifers feared the pro-choice rhetoric of the Democrat more than they feared the Republican's exceptions to the Sixth Commandment. The Republican candidate could count on the endorsement of pro-lifers because, at worst, he was "the lesser of two evils," and he was more likely to win some moderates by justifying abortion in some cases. If a politician is willing to sacrifice God's law on the altar of pragmatism and expedience, however, he may gain more votes—but at what cost? When we abandon God's law for a counterfeit standard of right and wrong, do we lose the favor of the only Voter that counts for eternity? When we support such candidates, how do we not bring bloodguilt on ourselves?

The Arguments for Exceptions

What about the Health of the Mother?
What about Rape and Incest?

What about a Severely Handicapped Fetus?

We should never abandon our principles in our response to these difficult, heart-wrenching scenarios. These exceptions can and should be answered without shame or hesitation from the unshakeable foundation of these two indisputable premises:

1. Human life begins at fertilization, and

2. It is always wrong to intentionally kill an innocent human being.

Scientific fact can prove the first premise conclusively. Nothing after fertilization makes you any more human or any more alive than the moment before. The Scripture says that Rebecca's twins "struggled together within her." Mary was "great with child." Job spoke of "a man child was conceived." Exodus 21 prescribed the death penalty for killing an unborn child through negligent carelessness. A fair trial and conviction for a capital crime was necessary before a person could be killed.

A murderer of one person is no less a murderer if he allows thousands to live, nor even if he saves thousands from dying.

Abortion Compounds Rape Violence

These exceptions, when evaluated, are really just smoke and mirrors—distractions from the true point of contention. If I held an infant in my arms and informed a crowd of pro-choice leaders that the child was conceived through rape, was handicapped, and the mother was extremely depressed that this child was still living, do you think any of them would propose that the infant should be killed? This proves that the circumstances surrounding conception are irrelevant, and making such excuses for abortion are insincere attempts to distract from the true point of contention in the debate: *when does life begin?*

It is always wrong—without exception—to fatally discriminate against human lives on the basis of their age, place of residence, stage of development, health status, or circumstances of conception. It is always wrong to kill one innocent human being to alleviate the suffering of another human being. It is just as evil to kill a pre-born baby conceived through rape or incest as it would be to kill a toddler who was conceived by rape or incest. Children should not be executed for the crimes of their fathers. One act of violence or sexual assault against an innocent person is not remedied, but rather, compounded by another act of violence against another innocent person.

A murderer of one person is no less a murderer if he allows thousands to live, nor even if he saves thousands from dying! We should never be swayed from the unshakable foundation of God's law by emotional appeals that admittedly swell our eyes with tears. Truth, compassion, and the fear of God should prevent us from this fatal compromise.

What About the Life of the Mother?

This is the exception that most commonly seduces the sincere pro-lifer. Answers in Genesis (AiG) is a large Christian ministry that is well known for their Creation Museum in the Cincinnati area; they've earned the respect of genuine Christians all over the world for their defense of the biblical six-day creation, but on February 26, 2013, the Bible took a back seat in their pragmatic justification of child-killing. In their *Answers* magazine, Dr. Tommy Mitchell, a physician and speaker for AiG, wrote an article entitled, "Is Abortion Ever Justifiable?" In this article, Dr. Mitchell justifies the killing of babies in some circumstances. If a mother has aggressive leukemia and requires immediate chemotherapy "that is virtually certain to kill the unborn child," and if postponing chemotherapy is too risky for the mother, then, Dr. Mitchell argues, the doctor is justified in advising "immediate abortion."

Is this justification even compatible with the scientific facts? The chemotherapy necessary to save the life of the leukemia patient in Dr. Mitchell's hypothetical scenario would be *just as effective* whether the patient were pregnant or not. Dr. Mitchell expressed concern that the low platelet count common with some chemotherapeutic agents would be too risky if the woman underwent delivery, but would a surgical abortion mitigate that risk at all? Where is the evidence that killing that baby is necessary to save the life of his or her mother?

Most physicians recommend an abortion before they will prescribe chemotherapy, however, it is not to save the mother's life, but to protect themselves from litigation.

As reported in *The Lancet* medical journal in August 2012, the German Breast Group followed 413 pregnant cancer patients receiving chemotherapy, and found little to no evidence of negative health effects on their infants. Delay of cancer treatment did "not significantly affect disease free survival" in this study, and chemotherapy was found to be relatively safe after the first trimester.

When you examine the actual fetal health risks of maternal chemotherapy, it looks like killing babies isn't good healthcare after all.

Most physicians recommend an abortion before they will prescribe chemotherapy, however, it is not to save the mother's life, but to protect themselves from litigation. I have witnessed physicians withhold life-saving care from a pregnant mother unless she gets an abortion, not because the abortion was necessary to save the mother's life, but because their care or the medicine they planned to prescribe could have hurt or handicapped the baby and they feared a lawsuit.

Drs. Tommy Mitchell and Elizabeth Mitchell also brought up HELLP Syndrome and chorioamnionitis as justifications for abortion. Dr. Elizabeth Mitchell even said that she would be willing to do an abortion in such a scenario. The medical literature declares that in chorioamnionitis and HELLP Syndrome, "facilitating delivery" may be necessary to save the life of the mother. Can you facilitate delivery and not dismember the baby? Of course. Granted, the premature delivery may inadvertently result in the death of the child, but the physician should do everything in his power to save the mother and the baby. If the mother's life is truly threatened, then the premature delivery may be the best way to save the baby, not just mother, because if the mother dies so does the baby. If through our careful treatment of the mother's illness the unborn baby inadvertently dies or is injured, this is tragic, but, if it is unintentional, it is not unethical and is consistent with both the Hippocratic Oath and the law of God. The intentional killing of an unborn baby by an abortion, however, is a grievous violation of God's law.

Dr. Elizabeth Mitchell and Dr. Tommy Mitchell countered: if the premature delivery resulted in the death of the baby, then the outcome was the same: the baby dies just as if an abortion was committed. Therefore, they argued, we should do what is best for the mother, even if that means aborting the baby. Mark Looy, who co-founded AiG with Ken Ham, concurred with the Mitchells: since the outcome was the same, then the abortion was justified.

First of all, the outcome is not necessarily the same. If a baby was delivered prematurely, the baby may survive. The dates could have been wrong, and the baby may be further along than we thought. The record of the earliest surviving baby is 18 weeks, little Kenya King born in Orlando, Florida, in 1985, as reported by the *Orlando Sentinel*. However, if the baby is dismembered and extracted piece by piece with forceps, as is done via a Dilation & Extraction abortion on a mid-trimester baby, what are the child's chances of survival then? The outcomes are not always identical.

Just because the baby is likely to die through a natural delivery, that does not justify an intentional killing. For example, if a rescuer is venturing into a burning vehicle to try to save its injured occupants, and is only able to save one of the two occupants, is it justifiable for him to then take out his gun and shoot the occupant he was unable to save? Of course not! Intentionally killing those you were not able to save is never justified in healthcare. We have the technology and expertise to provide quality healthcare to a pregnant woman without intentionally killing her unborn baby, regardless of the severity of her disease.

Just because the outcome is the same, that doesn't make the acts morally equivalent.

It is self-evident that killing a baby by ripping him or her out piece by piece is quite a different thing than a prematurely delivered baby (delivered to save the life of the mother *and* the baby) dying peacefully in the arms of his parents in spite of physician's care. *Trying* to save a baby's life and failing is not morally equivalent to *trying to kill* a baby! An abortion violates God's law because it intends to kill an innocent person, whereas prematurely delivering a baby and trying to save his or her life does not intend to kill and does not violate God's law. One is violent and cruel, the other heroic and compassionate.

Pennsylvania abortionist Kermit Gosnell received "Guilty" verdicts for snipping the cervical spines of babies who survived his late-term abortion procedures.

A friend of mine last year saw their preborn baby miscarry; in spite of the physician's efforts, the baby died peacefully in her parents' arms.

Just because the outcome is the same, that doesn't make the acts morally equivalent.

Many Christian and pro-life groups concur that an abortion is never necessary to save the mother's life: the American Assn. of Pro-Life Ob/Gyns, the Christian Medical Association, Personhood USA and several state affiliates, the Catholic Medical Association, American Right to Life, both Georgia and Colorado Right to Life, and the Dublin Declaration, just to name a few.

The Dublin Declaration is a statement from physicians opposing the legalization of abortion in Ireland; they state,

> "As experienced practitioners and researchers in obstetrics and gynecology, we affirm that direct abortion—the purposeful destruction of the unborn child—is not medically necessary to save the life of a woman. We uphold that there is a fundamental difference between abortion and necessary medical treatments that are carried out to save the life of the mother, even if such treatment results in the loss of her unborn child."

[While] a premature delivery may be necessary to save the life of the mother, ... the physician should do everything possible to save the baby as well.

Congressman and obstetrician Ron Paul said he never saw an abortion that was medically necessary. Former Surgeon General Everett Koop said that abortion was "not needed to save the life of the mother." He wrote, "In my thirty-six years in pediatric surgery I have never known of one instance where the child had to be aborted to save the mother's life."

Even Planned Parenthood's Dr. Alan Guttmacher acknowledged, "Today it is possible for almost any patient to be brought through pregnancy alive, unless she suffers from a fatal illness such as cancer or leukemia, and, if so, abortion would be unlikely to prolong, much less save, life."

With their abortion justifications, Answers in Genesis leaders have abandoned the solid rock of God's Word for the quicksand of relative morality. They have surrendered their trump card—"Thus saith the Lord"—to the father of lies. Having sheathed the sword of the Spirit in the spiritual battle for souls and for freedom, they've handicapped themselves. They may have always been true to God's Word in the past, but like a faithful husband who makes an exception on a business trip with his secretary, they've made one fatal exception to the Sixth Commandment forbidding murder, thus bringing bloodguilt upon themselves for all who kill their children following their lead.

What About an Ectopic Pregnancy?

Dr. Elizabeth Mitchell also mentioned an ectopic pregnancy as a justification for abortion. An ectopic pregnancy is when the embryo attaches somewhere inside the mother's body in a place other than the inner lining of the uterus. Is an abortion in an ectopic pregnancy necessary to save the mother's life? Not at all.

What is rarely realized is that there are several cases in the medical literature where abdominal ectopic pregnancies have survived! There are no cases of ectopic pregnancies in a fallopian tube surviving, but it is well documented in the medical literature that a tubal ectopic pregnancy may unattach and re-attach in the uterus. There have also been successful embryo transplants where the embryo was surgically removed from the fallopian tube and implanted into the uterus. Regardless, several large studies have confirmed that expectant management may allow spontaneous regression of the tubal ectopic pregnancy the vast majority of the time.

If expectant management fails and the ectopic pregnancy does not spontaneously resolve, and surgery becomes necessary to save the life of the mother, it is likely at this point that the baby has already overgrown his or her blood supply and succumbed. Nevertheless, with the mother's life imminently threatened by the pregnancy, a premature delivery may be necessary to save the life of the mother, but the physician should do everything possible to save the baby as well.

A chemical abortion with a medicine called methotrexate is often recommended by physicians to mothers with early tubal ectopic pregnancies to decrease the chances of hemorrhage or a surgical alternative being necessary later. I have found this to be an unnecessary risk to human life. I offer the following true case to demonstrate this point.

One of my patients was diagnosed with a tubal ectopic pregnancy by her obstetrician, and he informed her that they were fortunate to have made the diagnosis early and that she should have a methotrexate abortion. The patient was strongly pro-life, and did not want to take the medicine, but the physician insisted. The baby was not going to survive, he argued, and a chemical abortion now could prevent the need for a surgical procedure later. The chemical abortion would lessen her chances of a life-threatening rupture of her fallopian tube. The chemical abortion was also better at preserving future fertility than surgical removal of the ectopic pregnancy later. Feeling like she had no other reasonable alternative, she took the methotrexate.

However, there was a complication. Two weeks later, she still had vaginal bleeding and pelvic discomfort. A repeat ultrasound confirmed the physician's worst fears: there was a pregnancy in the uterus! Either the patient had twins, one in the fallopian tube and one in the uterus, or the fallopian tube pregnancy unattached and reattached in the uterus.

If there were twins, expectant management would likely have seen spontaneous resolution of the tubal pregnancy or would have required surgical removal of the tubal pregnancy when the embryo was likely to be dead, but in both cases the uterine pregnancy would have survived. If the tubal pregnancy dislodged and reattached in the uterus, the baby would be alive today and the mother would not have suffered such guilt and life-threatening hemorrhaging.

Pro-Life Without Exceptions

In conclusion, there are no occasions in which an abortion is justified. None. Not even for the life of the mother. Scientific fact and God's Word are clear: life begins at conception (fertilization), and there are no exceptions to the Sixth Commandment forbidding the intentional killing of innocent people. We must stand true to these foundational principles through every emotional appeal and in every tragic scenario if we are to have any principles at all for which to stand.

Parental Consent Laws Protect Teens

Teresa S. Collett

Teresa S. Collett is a professor of law at the University of St. Thomas School of Law in Minneapolis.

On March 8 [2012], the U.S. House of Representatives Subcommittee on the Constitution heard testimony on the proposed Child Interstate Abortion Notification Act (CIANA). I was among those who testified in favor of the Act. CIANA would prohibit transporting a minor across state lines with the intent that she obtain an abortion without involving her parents as may be required by her home state. It also would require that abortion providers comply with the parental notification or consent laws of a minor's home state when performing an abortion on a non-resident minor. More controversially, CIANA would require 24 hours' notice to the girl's parents if she was not a resident in the state where the abortion is being performed. All of these requirements would be waived in the event of a medical emergency threatening the girl's life or if the girl certified that she was the victim of parental abuse.

The *New York Times* criticized the Act in an editorial titled "Yet Another Curb on Abortion." The editors called CIANA "mean-spirited," "constitutionally suspect," and "callous." It is none of these things. It is, in fact, a popular commonsense proposal that is fully constitutional.

Most Americans Support Parental Consent Laws

There is a national consensus in favor of parental involvement laws, notwithstanding the controversial nature of abortion

Teresa S. Collett, "Parental Consent Protects Young Women's Health," *Public Discourse*, Witherspoon Institute, March 29, 2012. Copyright © 2012 by the Witherspoon Institute. All rights reserved. Reproduced by permission.

laws more generally. For more than three decades, polls have consistently reflected that over 70 percent of Americans support parental consent laws. Most recently a Gallup Poll released July 25, 2011, showed that 71 percent of Americans support a law requiring parental consent prior to performance of an abortion on a minor. According to a 2009 Pew Research Poll "Even among those who say abortion should be legal in most or all cases, 71% favor requiring parental consent."

Forty-five states have passed laws requiring parental notice or consent, although only thirty-seven states' laws are in effect at the moment due to constitutional challenges by abortion rights activists. And the weakest of these laws allow notice to or consent by other adult relatives of girls seeking abortion.

Various reasons underlie the popular support of these laws. As [US Supreme Court] Justices [Sandra Day] O'Connor, [Anthony] Kennedy, and [David] Souter observed in *Planned Parenthood v. Casey* [in 1992], parental involvement laws for abortions "are based on the quite reasonable assumption that minors will benefit from consultation with their parents and that children will often not realize that their parents have their best interests at heart."

According to a national study conducted by researchers associated with Guttmacher, disappointment is the most common response of parents who learn that their teen daughter is pregnant, and almost no parent responds with violence.

The *New York Times* editorial disputed this claim, criticizing CIANA on the basis that teens "have reason to fear a violent reaction" and will "resort to unsafe alternatives."

These objections are repeatedly voiced by abortion activists. Yet they ignore published studies, many of them by the Guttmacher Institute, a research institute founded by Planned

Parenthood, demonstrating that less than half of pregnant teens tell their parents of their pregnancy and very few experience ill effects from the disclosure.

Few Teens Face More than Parental Disappointment

According to a national study conducted by researchers associated with Guttmacher, disappointment is the most common response of parents who learn that their teen daughter is pregnant, and almost no parent responds with violence. Teens reported an increase in parental stress as the most common consequence of disclosing their pregnancy. Less than half of one percent of the teens reported that they were "beaten."

The claim that minors will resort to unsafe alternatives is equally bogus. A 2007 study of self-induced medical abortions reported no cases involving children or adolescents. Similarly, notwithstanding the fact that parental involvement laws have been on the books in various states for over thirty years, there has been no case in which it has been established that a minor was injured as the result of obtaining an illegal or self-induced abortion in an attempt to avoid parental involvement.

What has been established, however, is that many teen pregnancies are the result of coercion and statutory rape. National studies reveal that almost two thirds of adolescent mothers have partners older than twenty years of age. In a study of over 46,000 pregnancies by school-age girls in California, researchers found that 71 percent, or over 33,000, were fathered by adult post-high-school men who were an average of five years older than the mothers. Perhaps even more shocking was the finding that men aged twenty-five years or older father more births among California school-age girls than do boys under age eighteen. Parental involvement laws are just one way the law can attempt to protect young girls from the predatory practices of some men.

Mandatory Reporting Laws

Mandatory reporting of statutory rape and other sex crimes is another. Yet as evidenced by recent news stories, some abortion providers refuse to comply with reporting laws. Instead of reporting underage sex to state authorities who can then investigate and protect a girl from future abuse, clinics intentionally remain ignorant of the circumstances giving rise to the pregnancy. Clinics in Kansas have even gone so far as to argue in federal court that twelve-year-old children have a right to keep their sexual activities private and thus reporting laws are unconstitutional. Thankfully this absurd claim was rejected, but only on appeal from a district court ruling embracing the clinics' argument.

In addition to providing some protection against sexual exploitation of minors, the Supreme Court has identified three ways in which teens may benefit medically from parental involvement. First, parents are more likely to have greater experience in selecting medical providers and thus be able "to distinguish the competent and ethical from those that are incompetent or unethical." This benefit should not be lightly ignored, as evidenced by the horrific practices engaged in by Kermit Gosnell in Philadelphia, an abortion provider currently being prosecuted for multiple murders in connection with his abortion practice.

Evidence shows that of all teens obtaining abortions, only a tiny fraction of one percent occur in emergency circumstances.

Second, parents can provide additional information about the minor's medical history—information a minor may not know, remember, or be willing to share. This can be particularly important where there is a history of depression or other mental disorder that may impact the minor's post-abortion psychological health. While claims of "post-abortion trauma" are hotly disputed, no one questions that women with a history of depression may be more susceptible to post-abortion mental health problems.

Finally, parents who know their daughter has undergone an abortion can more readily identify any post-procedure problems such as infection or hemorrhaging—two of the most common post-abortion complications. If caught early, both infection and hemorrhaging can be dealt with easily, but if ignored, either can lead to other complications or even death.

The Medical Emergency Objection

Opponents of CIANA argue that the Act would endanger teen health, and they criticize the emergency exception to parental involvement, which is limited to the life of the minor. This objection, like the other objections, ignores reality and constitutional precedents. In the five years between 2005 and 2010, the Wisconsin Department of Health reported almost 3,200 abortions performed on minors. Not a single one involved a medical emergency. During the same five years in Alabama, where over 4,500 abortions were performed on minors, only two involved a medical emergency. In Nebraska, of the 13,596 abortions performed on all women from 2005 to 2010, only three involved a medical emergency.

Evidence shows that of all teens obtaining abortions, only a tiny fraction of one percent occur in emergency circumstances. In *Gonzales v. Carhart*, the United States Supreme Court upheld the constitutionality of the federal partial-birth abortion ban that contained a similarly narrow emergency exception, in part because of evidence that no broader exception was necessary.

Independent of the fact that such emergencies are so rare, it is precisely in these circumstances, when a teen's life or health is threatened by a pregnancy, that parental involvement is most needed and most helpful.

Interstate Notification Law Is Necessary

It is beyond dispute that young girls are being taken to out-of-state clinics in order to procure secret abortions. Abortion clinic operators in states without parental involvement laws routinely advertise in neighboring states where clinics must obtain parental consent or provide parental notice. For example, abortion providers in Granite City, Illinois have advertised Illinois's absence of any parental involvement requirement to Missouri minors, which has a parental consent law, for decades.

Missouri legislators attempted to stop this practice by passing a law creating civil remedies for parents and their daughters against individuals who would "intentionally cause, aid, or assist a minor" in obtaining an abortion without parental consent or a judicial bypass. Abortion providers immediately attacked the law as unconstitutional, but it was upheld by the Missouri Supreme Court. The Court limited its opinion, however, by the observation that "Missouri simply does not have the authority to make lawful out-of-state conduct actionable here, for its laws do not have extraterritorial effect."

The proposed Child Interstate Abortion Notification Act is an appropriate and measured response to the limitations on state powers in our federalist system. It is grounded by the reality that parents are nearly always the first to help a teen in trouble, and that fact does not change when the "trouble" is an unplanned pregnancy. There is no other elective surgery that minors can obtain while keeping their parents in the dark, and the controversy surrounding this Act shows just how severely the judicial creation of abortion rights has distorted American law.

Conscience Laws Are Essential to Protect Health-Care Providers' Beliefs

Joxel García and Terry Michael Rauch II

Joxel García is a principal of the International Healthcare Solutions Group (IHSG), past president and dean of Ponce School of Medicine and Health Sciences, and former assistant secretary for health, US Department of Health and Human Services. Terry Michael Rauch II is a partner at IHSG.

As a medical student I was amazed by the experience of great beauty and love when a baby is delivered. In fact, one of the main reasons I became an obstetrician was for the privilege of helping a mother welcome her child into the world and into the life of her family. I wanted to share in those precious moments when the miracle of life and the grace of God can be felt in an incomparable way. So I decided to seek a residency program in obstetrics and gynecology.

In the months before graduation from medical school, students go through the residency interview process, one of the most exciting, and also career-defining, periods in one's professional life. It's the time when students visit various hospitals to learn more about their training programs and to be interviewed for the few residency slots available. My excitement turned to dismay as three training programs in the New York and New Jersey area offered me residency positions, but only on condition that I would learn to perform abortions during my training, despite my having informed them multiple times that performing abortions was against my Catholic faith and values. When I stood up for my beliefs I was told that I would not be eligible.

Several of my medical school friends encountered similar situations at other medical residency programs, but we didn't know what to do or what legal protection we had. Fortunately, I was successfully matched to a residency program that did not ask me to violate my beliefs.

Years later I learned that federal law prohibited those institutions from forcing medical personnel to perform abortions and other procedures against their conscience and faith. When I became the 13th United States Assistant Secretary for Health, I worked with numerous professionals and legal experts at the U.S. Department of Health and Human Services to help defend the constitutionally-protected rights of conscience of the many healthcare providers who are discriminated against because of their beliefs and ethical values. Over the years, I've met countless numbers of students, nurses, doctors, pharmacists and other healthcare providers who were or who are today confronted with the same dilemmas.

Catholic Health Care

Catholic healthcare providers have been leaders in the delivery of care in the United States and across the globe. There are over 600 Catholic hospitals in the United States alone. Catholic community hospitals represent one out of every eight hospitals and one-sixth of all patient admissions in the United States.

Faith-based professionals are being driven out of medicine, which in turn will also limit access for patients.

The establishment and growth of Catholic health care has a rich history beginning in 1823, when Catholic sisters first began staffing hospitals. These women manifested their love of God in the midst of their own hardships and suffering, while leading others to discover the love of Christ in suffering. Thus, they sought to integrate their care for the sick and dying with their spirituality.

Catholic faith-based health care has been and remains an integral part of our nation's health delivery system.

The Church Amendment

It is increasingly evident that there are efforts in our country to force medical providers to either perform actions against their personal conscience or leave the profession completely. Faith-based professionals are being driven out of medicine, which in turn will also limit access for patients.

Only robust legal protection of conscience rights will ensure the continued services of many Catholic medical professionals who are working tirelessly to heal and prevent illness.

The Supreme Court's 1973 *Roe v. Wade* decision gave new meaning to the need for conscientious objection. Following this decision many physicians, particularly Catholic doctors, refused to take part in procedures that would violate their moral or religious convictions.

Recognizing this real problem, Congress passed the Health Programs Extension Act of 1973, which included the Church Amendment.

Named after, and introduced by, Senator Frank Church, this amendment was the first federal legislation establishing a conscience clause in health care. It states that public officials may not require individuals or organizations who receive certain public funds to perform abortion or sterilization procedures, or to make facilities or personnel available for the performance of such procedures, if this "would be contrary to religious beliefs or moral convictions" (42 USC 300a-7). It remains in law today.

Other Federal Conscience Laws

Complementing the Church Amendment, the Coats Amendment was passed by Congress in 1996 to amend the Public Health Service Act. Named after Senator Dan Coats (R-IN), this amendment maintains federal funding and legal status of medical institutions that do not offer or refer for abortion training, and protects individuals who decline to receive such training.

A third federal conscience clause provision is the Weldon Amendment, named after Congressman Dave Weldon (R-FL). Signed into law in 2004, the Weldon Amendment prohibits federal agencies and programs, as well as state and local governments, from discriminating against healthcare entities because they do not offer abortion services or provide coverage or referral for abortions. The Weldon Amendment covers a diverse group of healthcare entities, including physicians and other healthcare providers, hospitals, provider-sponsored organizations, HMOs, insurance plans and any kind of healthcare facility, organization or plan.

Emerging moral stressors associated with proposed changes to our profession may have drastic repercussions on the level and quality of care we are able to provide.

It is also widely accepted, and guaranteed in law, that physicians, nurses and prison employees have a right to refuse to participate in executions for reasons of conscience.

Conscience Protection Creates Better Medical Professionals

Conscience protection also has critical implications for the performance of medical professionals.

As physicians and medical professionals we constantly confront moral dilemmas in our practice. Our work environment exists in an increasingly complex healthcare system with economic pressures as well as physician and nurse shortages. Emerging moral stressors associated with proposed changes to our profession may have drastic repercussions on the level and quality of care we are able to provide. Several studies have shown that it is important that caregivers work in accord with their moral convictions.

A 2009 descriptive study explored the relationship between moral distress and the performance and retention of medical professionals. The study concluded that moral distress played a significant role in whether a medical professional intends to continue practicing. A 2004 study found that emotional exhaustion is significantly related to moral distress.

The moment we allow our conscience to be replaced by a government "conscience," we begin to lose our freedom.

Finally, a Swedish study in 2008 examined factors related to stress and conscience in health care. It found that stress increased from not being able to follow one's conscience or deal with moral problems at work. In order for conscience and moral sensitivity to become an asset instead of a burden, healthcare employees need to be able to express their moral concerns.

A Spiritual Obligation

What the Second Vatican Council declared in *Dignitatis Humanae* is as true for medical professionals as it is for all of us:

> All are bound to follow their conscience faithfully in every sphere of activity so that they may come to God, who is their last end. Therefore, the individual must not be forced to act against conscience nor be prevented from acting according to conscience, especially in religious matters. The reason is because the practice of religion of its very nature consists primarily of those voluntary and free internal acts by which human beings direct themselves to God. Acts of this kind cannot be commanded or forbidden by any merely human authority.

As medical providers we do our very best to provide care and medical advice according to our knowledge and conscience to ensure that the patient is receiving appropriate care.

As a Catholic physician I have a spiritual obligation as well as a legal right to offer and perform clinical services that do not violate my ethical, moral, personal, or religious convictions or beliefs—in short, my conscience. As a doctor the freedom to practice based not only on scientific knowledge but also on my faith and conscience allows me and all physicians and healthcare providers to offer the best quality of medicine possible. As a patient, I want my doctors, nurses and other healthcare providers to offer the same type of care. The moment we allow our conscience to be replaced by a government "conscience," we begin to lose our freedom.

Abortion Can Save a Woman's Life

National Women's Law Center

The National Women's Law Center is a Washington, DC-based nonprofit that works to improve the lives of women and their families through litigation and policy initiatives.

This year [2013] marks the 40th anniversary of *Roe v. Wade*, the landmark Supreme Court ruling that affirmed a woman's right to a safe and legal abortion. Yet, anti-abortion opponents in the states continue to relentlessly attack this right. In 2012, states passed 43 restrictions on abortion, the second highest number of new abortion restrictions passed in a single year. These new obstacles to abortion represent a dangerous overreach into women's reproductive health care and personal medical decisions.

States Are Requiring Women to Undergo Medically Unnecessary, Physically Invasive Ultrasounds Before Obtaining an Abortion.

In 2012, one state (Virginia) enacted a provision requiring a woman to undergo an ultrasound before she can obtain an abortion. Although mandatory ultrasound bills were introduced in additional states in 2012, the public outcry over Virginia politicians' overreach helped to stop these other states from moving forward.

There are now eight states that require an abortion provider to perform an ultrasound on each woman seeking an abortion. These laws subject a woman seeking an abortion to a medically unnecessary, physically invasive procedure. Requiring doctors to perform ultrasounds without regard for the circumstances or the patient's wishes impairs the doctor-patient relationship and violates principles of medical ethics. Mandatory ultrasound laws represent a profound disrespect for women's decision making and the clinical judgment of doctors.

States Are Banning Abortion Altogether Earlier in Pregnancy Than Allowed, Ignoring an Individual Woman's Particular Circumstances.

In 2012, legislatures in three states (Arizona, Georgia, and Louisiana) enacted provisions that ban abortion at or beyond twenty weeks' gestation, with only the most narrow exceptions. The laws in Arizona and Georgia have been challenged, and courts have blocked the laws as the lawsuits proceed.

These blatantly unconstitutional laws—which now exist in six states—deprive a woman of her ability to make an extremely personal, medical decision. Every pregnancy is different. These laws take the decision away from a woman and her doctor, and hand it over to politicians.

Abortion and Health Insurance

States Are Banning Insurance Coverage of Abortion, Taking Away Benefits Women Currently Have and Jeopardizing Women's Health.

In 2012, four states (Alabama, South Carolina, South Dakota, and Wisconsin) passed laws banning insurance coverage of abortion in the exchanges that will be established in the state as part of implementing the health care law. In one state (Michigan) a ban on insurance coverage of abortion in all private plans passed the legislature, but was vetoed by Governor Snyder, who pointed out the problems of intruding into the private market and not allowing coverage to protect women's health or in cases of rape and incest.

Twenty states now prevent women from obtaining insurance coverage for abortion services. Bans on insurance coverage of abortion represent a radical departure from the status quo. Most Americans with employer-based insurance currently have coverage for abortion, so these bans on coverage will result in a woman losing benefits she currently has. Bans on insurance coverage of abortion are also dangerous to women's health. A woman with a serious, permanent, and even life-shortening health condition will not be able to obtain insurance coverage for a medically necessary abortion. For example, a woman for whom continuing the pregnancy will result in permanent damage to her health, such as damage to her heart, lungs, or kidneys, or a pregnant woman who is diagnosed with cancer and must undergo chemotherapy will not have insurance coverage for these medically necessary abortions.

In 2012, four state legislatures (Arizona, Michigan, Mississippi, and Tennessee) passed targeted regulations of abortion providers (TRAP laws), in an attempt to shut down abortion providers in the state.

TRAP Laws and Funding Cuts

States Are Attempting to Regulate Abortion Providers Out of Existence.

In 2012, four state legislatures (Arizona, Michigan, Mississippi, and Tennessee) passed targeted regulations of abortion providers (TRAP laws), in an attempt to shut down abortion providers in the state. In one state (Minnesota), the governor vetoed a TRAP law passed by the legislature. TRAP laws require abortion providers to comply with medically unnecessary, burdensome requirements, such as widths of hallways or minimum square footage. Mississippi's law requires doctors that provide abortions to have admitting privileges at a local hospital, but doctors who provide abortions in the sole abortion clinic in the state have been denied privileges at every hospital to which they have applied. This law has been challenged in court.

States are Defunding Planned Parenthood.

In 2012, two states (AZ, NC) passed restrictions that effectively prevent Planned Parenthood clinics in the state from receiving certain family planning funds. Nine states now have such laws. These laws are part of a targeted campaign to shut down the health centers, jeopardizing not only women's access to safe, legal abortion, but also to basic, preventive health care like well-woman exams, screening for diabetes and high blood pressure, and testing for sexually transmitted infections.

Rural Women Are Hit Especially Hard

States Are Limiting Women's Access to Medication Abortion.

Three states in 2012 (Michigan, Oklahoma, and Wisconsin) passed laws that prohibit the use of telemedicine for medication abortion. One additional state—Minnesota—passed a similar law, but Governor Mark Dayton vetoed the bill. Seven states now ban the use of telemedicine for medication abortion. The use of telemedicine is an increasingly routine part of medical care that helps to improve access for individuals in rural areas who would not otherwise be able to easily and consistently access health services. Abortion providers similarly are trying to use telemedicine to provide access to abortion. Yet, these laws are designed to end the use of telemedicine for medication abortion, particularly harming women who live in rural areas where abortion providers are few and far between.

States Are Enacting Onerous New Mandatory Delay Requirements.

One state in 2012 (Utah) imposed an onerous new requirement that women wait 72 hours between receiving state-mandated counseling and receiving an abortion.

Twenty-six states require a woman to wait a specific amount of time before she can obtain an abortion. Such mandatory delays are an additional burden for women, especially women who must struggle to get time off from work or to pay for needless child-care costs, and rural women, who often have to travel hours to reach the closest health care provider.

As the attacks on women's access to reproductive health care continue unabated, the ability of women to obtain the health care they need has never been at greater risk. Politicians need to stop playing politics with women's health.

Denying Abortion Revictimizes Women Who Have Been Raped

Tara Culp-Ressler

Tara Culp-Ressler is the health editor for ThinkProgress, *a blog site published by the Center for American Progress, a progressive public policy research and advocacy organization.*

Americans overwhelmingly favor legal abortion access for victims of sexual assault. But their lawmakers are consistently refusing to enact policies in line with that.

According to an analysis conducted by the National Women's Law Center (NWLC), more than 70 percent of the new abortion restrictions enacted in the first half of 2013 don't include any kind of exemption for pregnancies that result from rape. And state lawmakers proposed even more measures to limit rape victims' abortion access that didn't make it into law—the NWLC's report finds that 86 percent of the anti-abortion bills proposed during the same time period didn't have a rape exception.

U.S. Congress didn't have a much better record during the first six months of the year. Seventy two percent of the bills proposed on a national level would have restricted abortion access even for rape victims.

The anti-abortion measures that apply to rape victims range from forcing a woman who has become pregnant from sexual assault to carry the pregnancy to term; to requiring her to look at an ultrasound of the fetus and listen to a fetal heartbeat; to banning her from using her own insurance coverage to pay for an abortion; to allowing hospitals to deny her abortion care.

Lack of Exception Is Deliberate

And the decision to omit a rape exception was certainly intentional in some states. One anti-abortion measure introduced in Mississippi stated: "The State of Mississippi shall not punish the crime of sexual assault with the death penalty, and neither shall persons conceived through a sexual assault be punished with the loss of his or her life."

The organization surveyed state-level and national legislation between January and May, so their data isn't comprehensive for the entire year. But many state legislatures concluded their sessions at the beginning of the summer and slowed down their flurry of anti-choice proposals (with a few notable exceptions).

State legislatures proposed more than 300 measures intended to limit access to abortion in the first half of the year—making 2013 one of the worst years for reproductive freedom in recent history.

Over the past year, abortion opponents have incited considerable controversy by making callous statements about rape victims. A year ago, former Rep. Todd Akin (R-MO) asserted that women don't often get pregnant from rape because the female body "has ways to try to shut that whole thing down." Since then, Republican politicians have suggested that pregnancies from rape are a "gift from God," mocked rape exceptions as "little gotcha amendments," and suggested abortion access for rape victims is unnecessary because ending a pregnancy will "put more violence on a woman's body." At least five GOP candidates who made insensitive comments about rape and abortion lost their seats in the 2012 election. The political firestorm became such a problem for the GOP that House Republicans ended up attending training programs to learn how to better talk about rape.

Onerous Requirements

However, that training hasn't translated into policy action. Even in rare cases when anti-abortion legislation does include a provision to ensure that rape victims will be able to access reproductive health care, the stringent guidelines can pose obstacles that render the exception meaningless. Rape victims are often required to report the crime—in some cases, within the first 48 hours—and provide specific details about their assailant to law enforcement. One Indiana bill introduced this year would have even required survivors of sexual assault to get the crime "verified" in order to access abortion care.

NWLC only considered abortion-related measures that could have included a specific exception for victims of sexual assault. That means the organization's report doesn't include any of the legislation that indirectly impacts women's abortion access, like laws imposing harsh regulations on abortion clinics that will force them to close. When taking into account the comprehensive landscape of abortion restrictions, state legislatures proposed more than 300 measures intended to limit access to abortion in the first half of the year—making 2013 one of the worst years for reproductive freedom in recent history.

Conscience Laws Deprive Women of Vital Health-Care Services

Amelia Thomson-DeVeaux

Amelia Thomson-DeVeaux is a writing fellow at the American Prospect, *a bimonthly liberal political magazine.*

In January [2014], two legislators in Virginia's House of Delegates introduced a bill that should have been uncontroversial. The bulk of HB 612 created new rules for genetic counselors practicing in the state, who had been unregulated and unlicensed. The roughly 95 genetic counselors already working in the state, screening pregnant women and adults for serious inheritable conditions, favored the law, which they saw as an extra layer of patient protection. The bill was so innocuous that by the time it passed in the House in late February, no one seemed to have noticed that it contained a conscience clause so sweeping that could allow counselors to refuse to provide fetal test results for conditions like Down Syndrome or Tay-Sachs Disease—the information patients came to them for in the first place—if they believed it could cause a woman to terminate her pregnancy.

Originally, the bill had only created a loophole for genetic counselors who want to refrain from offering information about abortion. These types of conscience clauses are typical in reproductive medicine—think of pharmacists refusing to provide birth control. They are, however, a significant concession for genetics counselors, since one of their primary tasks is to screen pregnant women for fetal abnormalities. Later, a

House subcommittee broadened the language to protect genetic counselors from legal retaliation if they refused to participate in counseling that violated their religious beliefs.

Wide-Ranging Consequences

By the time the bill hit the Senate, a coalition of left-leaning organizations led by the ACLU [American Civil Liberties Union] of Virginia, alarmed by the conscience clause's wide scope, were ready to fight. In their view, the language not only allowed genetic counselors to refuse to work with gay or unwed couples; it protected them if they withheld serious test results from pregnant women. Advocates from the ACLU and other abortion rights groups urged the Senate to weaken the language, but its sponsor—Janet Howell, a pro-choice Democrat—rebuffed them. In late March, Virginia's Democratic governor, Terry McAuliffe, signed the bill into law with the conscience clause intact, to the indignation of his liberal allies.

The focus [of genetic counseling] is above all on the client and her situation, not on what an individual counselor believes is right or wrong.

Genetic counseling is a relatively young profession with only a few thousand practitioners and little institutional clout. Virginia is only the fifteenth state to license them. They were peripheral to the fracas there, which pitted the conservative Family Foundation against the ACLU and its allies. (Neither group cared whether the counselors should be licensed: Debate revolved around the religious-freedom loophole, which mirrored efforts in other states to allow organizations to refuse to serve gay and lesbian customers.) But the passage of the Virginia law raises the possibility that conscience clauses may become par for the course as genetic counselors seek legitimacy in states.

Counselors Are Not Abortion Advocates

Genetic counselors have struggled for years to dislodge the notion that they advocate for abortion with their clients, but part of their job is to counsel pregnant women about all of their options. In the case of severe fetal abnormalities, that invariably includes a discussion of termination. Joel Frader, a professor of medical humanities at Northwestern University, believes that unless genetic counselors restrict their practice to screening adults for cancer or Huntington's Disease, abortion needs to be part of their professional lexicon. "If you're in the business of neonatal genetic counseling and you're uncomfortable talking about abortion, you don't need a conscience clause," he says. "You need to think about whether you should find a new profession."

In 2012, presidential candidate Rick Santorum declared that 90 percent of fetuses with Down Syndrome are aborted. There is no comprehensive data on how many pregnant women who are diagnosed with fetal abnormalities choose abortion, but claims like Santorum's have become a rallying cry on the right. Anti-choice advocates contend that abortions for fetal anomalies amount to eugenics. Early in 2013, one of these groups, Americans United for Life, released model legislation that would criminalize abortion in cases of sex selection and genetic abnormality. The laws were introduced in a handful of states—including North Dakota, Indiana, and Missouri—although only North Dakota's passed. Two of the states that have licensed genetic counselors—Oklahoma and Nebraska—have conscience clauses that allow them to refuse to provide information about abortion. In Rhode Island, a licensure bill died in committee after the ACLU insisted that its conscience clause be removed.

Genetics and Eugenics

The sometimes-unsavory history of genetic counseling doesn't make combating these criticisms any easier. Genetic counseling emerged in the late 1940s and early 1950s, driven by scientists intent on improving the human gene pool. Although some early counselors had qualms about their colleagues' enthusiasm for discouraging procreation among couples who might produce children with genetic defects, others were all too comfortable with the idea of playing God. The psychiatrist Franz Kallmann, one of the founders of the American Society of Human Genetics, once observed that "persons requesting genetic advice cannot always be presumed to be capable of making a realistic decision as to the choice of a mate, or the advisability of parenthood, without support in the form of directive guidance and encouragement." The role of the genetic counselor, in his view, was to shape humanity's genetic future by promoting ideal reproductive partnerships and discouraging those unfortunates in genetically imperfect unions from producing offspring.

A conscience clause doesn't seem too much to ask in exchange for gaining a regulatory framework.

This eugenic view persisted into the 1970s, when genetic counselors, shocked by Congressional hearings on the Tuskegee syphilis study and the involuntary sterilization of thousands of poor and minority women over the previous decade, began to reconsider their ethical approach. New codes of professional ethics emphasized patient autonomy and reproductive choice. In 1979, The National Society of Genetic Counselors was founded; from the start, it supported women's rights to end—or not to end—a pregnancy. Their statement on reproductive freedom also emphasizes women's right to use information from genetic testing to prepare for the needs of children with genetic problems. Many genetic counselors began to resist the notion that they were abortion pushers. "The focus is above all on the client and her situation, not on what an individual counselor believes is right or wrong," says Alexandra Minna Stern, a medical historian at the University of Michigan.

Misperceptions Abound

The specter of its eugenic past continues to haunt the profession, feeding the misperception that abortion is its customary prescription for birth defects or genetic disabilities. Susan Hassed, the director of the University of Oklahoma's genetic counseling program, promoted the state's licensure law, which passed in 2005. She says that abortion was frequently mentioned during the legislature's debates; the law ultimately included a conscience clause. "It was a little aggravating because our job is not selling termination," Hassed says. "People who see genetic counselors during pregnancy are not looking for an excuse to terminate. They're wanted pregnancies."

In the states where conscience clauses are already ensconced in their licensing statutes, genetic counselors are sanguine about the laws' effects. A conscience clause doesn't seem too much to ask in exchange for gaining a regulatory framework. "I'm a pragmatist," Hassed says. "Of course I'd like it if the law were simpler. But licensure is important because it protects the public from people who could provide incorrect information. I don't think people would go into genetic counseling wanting to do harm." Genetic counselors, mostly younger women who support reproductive rights, are not inclined to take advantage of a conscience clause anyway, Stern says. She warns, though, that could change. "You've seen the rise of pregnancy consultation services with a strong pro-life bent," she says. "Conscience clauses would open it up to counselors who might never refer anyone for an abortion."

Late-Term Abortion Bans

Even if the conscience clauses don't pose an immediate problem, genetic counselors may find their work stymied by another strain of anti-choice restriction: bans on abortion after

20 weeks. Disorders caused by genetic abnormalities often can't be detected until the second trimester of pregnancy. As a result, many of the pregnant women who are diagnosed with fetal abnormalities and choose to terminate their pregnancy don't seek an abortion until after the 20-week cutoff. Seven of the states that now ban abortion after that include no exception for fetal anomalies. Georgia, Louisiana, Texas, and Utah allow exemptions only for *lethal* anomalies, effectively prohibiting abortion after 20 weeks for diagnoses like Down Syndrome. These restrictions force genetic counselors to send patients seeking abortion after 20 weeks to clinics outside the state, a stressful and expensive process.

If anti-choice legislation continues to impinge on their practice, genetic counselors may have no choice but to go on the offensive to avoid seeing these laws undermine their code of ethics. "A broad range of reproductive health care options aren't negotiable in this field," Stern says. "They need to be legal and available."

Organizations to Contact

The editors have compiled the following list of organizations concerned with the issues debated in this book. The descriptions are derived from materials provided by the organizations. All have publications or information available for interested readers. The list was compiled on the date of publication of the present volume; the information here may change. Be aware that many organizations take several weeks or longer to respond to inquiries, so allow as much time as possible.

Americans United for Life (AUL)
310 South Peoria St., Suite 500, Chicago, IL 60607
(312) 568-4700 • fax: (312) 568-4747
website: www.aul.org

Founded in August 1971 prior to the *Roe v. Wade* Supreme Court decision, Americans United for Life (AUL) is the nation's oldest pro-life organization. AUL promotes pro-life ideals and policies from a nondenominational, interdisciplinary perspective. The organization believes that abortion harms women, men, and society in general and should be banned at the federal level. Information about current local and national abortion legislation is available on the AUL website along with details about ongoing pro-life activities sponsored by the organization.

BlackGenocide.org
PO Box 157, Montclair, NJ 07042
(866) 242-4997
e-mail: revchildress@yahoo.com
website: www.blackgenocide.org

Founded by Pastor Clenard H. Childress Jr. in September 2002, BlackGenocide.org works to ensure that the African American community in the United States has the opportunity to thrive and that Christian values serve as the basis for engaging in debate about bioethical issues. The organization's website provides information about the disproportionate number of black women who seek abortions and suggests that the procedure is promoted within minority communities as a means of population control. An extensive collection of articles and commentary about abortion in the black community are available from the site.

Center for Bio-Ethical Reform (CBR)

PO Box 219, Lake Forest, CA   92609
(949) 206-0600
e-mail: info@cbrinfo.org
website: www.abortionno.org

The Center for Bio-Ethical Reform (CBR) is a California-based nonprofit that seeks to expose the injustice of abortion by sharing graphic images of the procedure. The organization's ultimate goal is a nationwide ban on abortion. The CBR website offers educational resources and information about the group's various anti-abortion campaigns and features highly graphic photos and videos of aborted fetuses and abortion procedures.

Guttmacher Institute

125 Maiden Lane, 7th Floor, New York, NY
(800) 355-0244 • fax: (212) 248-1951
website: www.guttmacher.org

The Guttmacher Institute's integrated program of social science research, public education, and policy analysis serves as the basis for the advancement of sexual and reproductive health for women and men around the globe. The Institute welcomes the opinions and research of outside experts and encourages public debate about international health issues. Specific goals of the organization include helping men and women to make responsible family planning decisions, reducing the incidence of sexually transmitted disease, and ensuring that all women have access to safe abortions. Official publications of the organization include *Perspectives on Sexual and*

Reproductive Health, International Perspectives on Sexual and Reproductive Health, and *Guttmacher Policy Review,* all published quarterly. Archives of these journals can be accessed online along with additional reports and information.

NARAL Pro-Choice America

1156 15th St. NW, Suite 700, Washington, DC 20005
(202) 973-3000 • fax: (202) 973-3096
website: www.prochoiceamerica.org

Founded in 1969 as the National Association for the Repeal of Abortion Laws, NARAL Pro-Choice America is an advocate for women's reproductive rights. The organization works to ensure these rights are protected by supporting pro-choice policies and politicians; publishing information about abortion, birth control, and other reproduction topics; and organizing pro-choice campaigns at the grassroots level. Information about current activities as well as general information about abortion-related topics can be accessed on NARAL's website.

National Abortion Federation (NAF)

1660 L St. NW, Suite 450, Washington, DC 20036
(202) 667-5881 • fax: (202) 667-5890
e-mail: naf@prochoice.org
website: www.prochoice.org

As the professional organization of abortion providers in the United States, the National Abortion Federation (NAF) supports health professionals by providing training and other services to help ensure that women have the best available information and care when making decisions about their reproductive health. NAF is pro-choice and believes that it is a woman's right to make decisions about her health and body without the interference of government regulations or mandates. The Federation publishes guidelines for abortion providers, educational materials for the public, and current research and policy analysis concerning abortion and women's health issues. Copies of these materials and other resources are available for purchase and download from the organization's website.

National Organization for Women (NOW)

1100 H St. NW, 3rd Floor, Washington, DC   20005
(202) 628-8669 • fax: (202) 785-8576
website: www.now.org

The National Organization for Women (NOW) is a progressive feminist advocacy organization that works to combat all forms of discrimination in the United States to ensure that women have the chance to participate fully in society and enjoy rights, responsibilities, and opportunities equal to men. Specifically, the organization addresses issues such as abortion and reproductive rights, economic justice, and ending sex discrimination. NOW believes that safe and legal abortion should be available to all women without government restriction because reproductive rights are issues of life and death. Information about NOW's current reproductive rights campaigns can be read online along with fact sheets and other educational publications.

National Personhood Alliance (NPA)

783 Holcomb Bridge Rd., Norcross, GA   30071
(770) 339-6880
website: www.personhood.net

The National Personhood Alliance (NPA) is a Bible-based confederation of organizations and pro-life leaders who believe that establishing personhood for fertilized eggs is an essential part of enacting laws that protect the sanctity of life from conception to natural death. The organization's website includes information about the Personhood movement and the bioethical issues that it intersects with: abortion, in vitro fertilization, contraception, artificial reproductive technologies, cloning, stem cell research, eugenics, disabilities, artificial intelligence and robotics, aging, euthanasia, trans-humanism, and other concerns.

National Right to Life Committee (NRLC)

512 10th St. NW, Washington, DC   20004
(202) 626-8800
e-mail: NRLC@nrlc.org
website: www.nrlc.org

The National Right to Life Committee (NRLC) was formed in 1973 following the Supreme Court's decision in *Roe v. Wade* federally legalizing abortion in the United States. The NRLC believes that human life should be protected from the time of conception forward and hopes to one day see the *Roe* decision overturned with a federal abortion ban. The organization advocates pro-life policies by lobbying Congress and providing information to the public about the horrors of abortion. *National Right to Life News* is the monthly publication of the NRLC, and current as well as past issues can be read online.

Pew Research Center (PRC)

1615 L St. NW, Suite 700, Washington, DC   20036
(202) 419-4300 • fax: (202) 419-4349
website: www.pewresearch.org

The Pew Research Center (PRC) is a nonpartisan research organization that informs the public about the issues, attitudes, and trends shaping America and the world. It conducts public opinion polling, demographic research, media content analysis, and other empirical social science research. Pew Research does not take policy positions; it is a subsidiary of the Pew Charitable Trusts, an independent nonprofit research organization. PRC has examined and reported on various aspects of the abortion issue and its website features hundreds of publications related to the topic, including a wide variety of fact sheets, reports, surveys, and studies.

Planned Parenthood Federation of America (PPFA)

434 West 33rd St., New York, NY   10001
(212) 541-7800 • fax: (212) 245-1845
website: www.plannedparenthood.org

The Planned Parenthood Federation of America (PPFA) provides reproductive health-care and information about options for family planning and sex education to individuals, and aid to organizations with similar missions worldwide. The organization works through its local offices around the United States to offer affordable services and products to prevent and deal with unintended pregnancy as well as sexually transmitted diseases. Planned Parenthood is the largest provider of abortion in the United States and has always been an advocate of pro-choice policies. The organization's website provides information on the safety of abortion and the importance of continuing to keep abortion legal in the United States. In addition to abortion issues, the Planned Parenthood website contains information about health topics such as birth control, emergency contraception, and sexually transmitted diseases and other key issues such as global reproductive rights and sex education programs that are not abstinence-only approaches.

Population Connection

2120 L St. NW, Suite 500, Washington, DC   20037
(202) 332-2200 • fax: (202) 332-2302
e-mail: info@populationconnection.org
website: www.populationconnection.org

Formerly Zero Population Growth, Population Connection educates people about the dangers of the world's growing population and offers methods to stabilize the global population. Among other issues, the organization focuses on women's reproductive health as a means to control population growth, promoting access to family planning programs, pro-choice policies, and alternatives to abstinence-only sex education worldwide. Population Connection's official magazine is *The Reporter*, published triannually. Electronic archives of this publication and other reports and fact sheets are available on the organization's website.

Priests for Life

PO Box 141172, Staten Island, NY   10314

(718) 980-4400 • fax: (718) 980-6515
e-mail: mail@priestsforlife.org
website: www.priestsforlife.org

Priests for Life was formed with the goal of vocally and actively opposing abortion and euthanasia worldwide. Additionally, the organization promotes the belief that abortion is murder with hopes that eventually the practice will be banned. Priests for Life has founded programs such as Silent No More, which seeks to publicize the devastating effects of abortion on men and women as well as their extended families. Other projects of the organization include publicizing graphic images of aborted fetuses as well as abortion procedures to convince the American people that the practice should be banned. These pictures as well as additional information about abortion can be accessed on the Priests for Life website.

United States Conference of Catholic Bishops (USCCB)
3211 4th St. NE, Washington, DC   20017
(202) 541-3000
website: www.usccb.org

The United States Conference of Catholic Bishops (USCCB) opposes abortion, and the promotion of pro-life policies is at the center of the organization's advocacy efforts worldwide. USCCB provides extensive information about abortion on its website, including church documents and teachings, articles and publications, as well as testimony and letters. Specific abortion-related issues addressed by the organization include the Freedom of Choice Act, partial-birth abortion, and international abortion issues.

World Health Organization (WHO)
Avenue Appia 20, Geneva 27   1211
   Switzerland
+ 41 22 791 21 11 • fax: + 41 22 791 31 11
e-mail: info@who.int
website: www.who.int

The World Health Organization (WHO) is the United Nations's specialized agency for health. Established in 1948, WHO seeks to promote the highest possible level of health for all people, defined as a state of complete physical, mental, and social well-being and not merely the absence of disease or infirmity. WHO's website contains a library of the organization's reports and publications, as well as links to various world health journals and other resources. Abortion-related publications include "Preventing Unsafe Abortion" and "Emergency Contraception: Dispelling the Myths and Misperceptions."

Bibliography

Books

Randy C. Alcorn   *Why Pro-Life? Caring for the Unborn and Their Mothers.* Peabody, MA: Hendrickson, 2012.

Jennifer Baumgardner   *Abortion and Life.* New York: Akashic, 2008.

Daniel Becker   *Personhood: A Pragmatic Guide to Pro-Life Victory in the 21st Century.* Alpharetta, GA: TKS Publications, 2011.

Francis J. Beckwith   *Defending Life: A Moral and Legal Case Against Abortion Choice.* New York: Cambridge University Press, 2007.

Sarah Erdreich   *Generation Roe: Inside the Future of the Pro-Choice Movement.* New York: Seven Stories, 2013.

Clarke D. Forsythe   *Abuse of Discretion: The Inside Story of* Roe v. Wade. New York: Encounter, 2013.

Merle Hoffman   *Intimate Wars: The Life and Times of the Woman Who Brought Abortion from the Back Alley to the Board Room.* New York: Feminist Press, 2012.

N.E.H. Hull and Peter Charles Hoffer	Roe v. Wade: *The Abortion Rights Controversy in American History*, 2nd ed. Lawrence: University Press of Kansas, 2010.
Abby Johnson	*Unplanned: The Dramatic True Story of a Former Planned Parenthood Leader's Eye-Opening Journey Across the Life Line.* Carol Stream, IL: Tyndale Momentum, 2011.
Patricia Miller	*Good Catholics: The Battle over Abortion in the Catholic Church.* Berkeley: University of California Press, 2014.
Cristina Page	*How the Pro-Choice Movement Saved America: Freedom, Politics and the War on Sex.* New York: Basic Books, 2006.
Rickie Solinger	*Reproductive Politics: What Everyone Needs to Know.* New York: Oxford University Press, 2013.
Michael Tooley et al.	*Abortion: Three Perspectives.* New York: Oxford University Press, 2009.
Susan Wicklund and Alan S. Kesselheim	*This Common Secret: My Journey as an Abortion Doctor.* New York: PublicAffairs, 2008.
Joshua Wilson	*The Street Politics of Abortion: Speech, Violence, and America's Culture Wars.* Palo Alto, CA: Stanford Law Books, 2013.

Periodicals and Internet Sources

Charlene Aaron "Pro-Life Leaders Mourn Black Genocide," Christian Broadcasting Network, February 28, 2011. www.cbn.com.

AbortionFacts.com "Fact #18: Abortion Disproportionally Targets Minority Babies," 2014. www.abortionfacts.com.

Amy Allina et al. "Pre-Existing Conditions: How Restrictions on Abortion Coverage and Marginalization of Care Paved the Way for Discriminatory Treatment of Abortion in Health Reform and Beyond," Center for Women Policy Studies, August 2012. http://centerwomenpolicy.org.

Laura Bassett "Anti-Abortion Laws Take Dramatic Toll on Clinics Nationwide," *Huffington Post*, November 11, 2013. www.huffingtonpost.com.

Daniel Burke "Six Surprising Changes to the Anti-Abortion March for Life," CNN, January 21, 2014. http://religion.blogs.cnn.com.

Aaron E. Carroll "How Hobby Lobby Ruling Could Limit Access to Birth Control," *New York Times*, June 30, 2014.

David Crary "Abortion in Cases of Rape Dividing Pro-Life Movement," *Southeast Missourian*, April 13, 2014. www.semissourian.com.

Lizzie Crocker "Pro-Lifers Descend on UN, Decrying Abortion as an 'Act of Violence,'" Daily Beast, March 8, 2013. www.thedailybeast.com.

Tara Culp-Ressler "Scientists Studying 'Fetal Pain' Don't Actually Want Their Research to Justify Abortion Bans," *Think Progress*, September 17, 2013. http://thinkprogress.org.

Daily Beast "The Geography of Abortion Access," January 22, 2013. www.thedailybeast.com.

Daily Beast "*Roe v. Wade* Turns 40," January 2013. www.thedailybeast.com.

Erik Eckholm "Abortions Declining in US, Study Finds," *New York Times*, February 3, 2014.

Juliet Eilperin "So Abortion Will Be an Issue in 2014. Where Could It Make a Difference?," *Washington Post*, July 8, 2013.

Susan Estrich "The Abortion Fight—40 Years Later," *Courier*, April 3, 2014.

Guttmacher Institute "Restricting Insurance Coverage of Abortion, State Policies in Brief," March 2014. www.guttmacher.org.

Nicco Hines "How Widespread Is Sex-Selective Abortion?," Daily Beast, January 16, 2014. www.thedailybeast.com.

Bari Hussain and Ishrat Zerin	"Is Abortion a Human Right for Women?," *Daily Star*, August 6, 2013.
Pete Kasperowicz	"House Votes to Limit Abortion Coverage Under Affordable Care Act," *The Hill*, January 28, 2014. http://thehill.com.
Neil King Jr.	"Late-Term Abortion Bans Have Support," *Wall Street Journal*, July 24, 2013.
Anu Kumar	"Do US Abortion Restrictions Violate Human Rights?," *Huffington Post*, October 25, 2011. www.huffingtonpost.com.
Joshua Lang	"What Happens to Women Who Are Denied Abortions?," *New York Times*, June 12, 2013.
Alexandra Le Tellier	"Are Women Stupid? New Texas Abortion Bill Treats Them That Way," *Los Angeles Times*, July 31, 2013.
Dana Liebelson and Sydney Brownstone	"Imagine You Were Raped. Got Pregnant. Then Your Rapist Sought Custody," *Mother Jones*, August 24, 2012.
Adam Liptak	"Supreme Court Rejects Contraceptives Mandate for Some Corporations," *New York Times*, June 30, 2014.
David Masci	"The New Legal Battlefield over Abortion," Pew Research Center, July 31, 2013. www.pewresearch.org.

Kate Michelman   "Long Road Since 'Roe,'" Philly.com, April 23, 2014. www.philly.com.

R. Albert Mohler Jr.   "Why the Abortion Issue Won't Go Away," CNN, January 23, 2012. http://religion.blogs.cnn.com.

Andrew Napolitano   "Is Rape a Moral Justification for Abortion?," *Reason*, August 23, 2012.

NARAL Pro-Choice America   "Congress Should Not Legitimize the Mythical 'Post-Abortion Syndrome,'" January 1, 2014. www.prochoice america.org.

NARAL Pro-Choice America   "Mandatory Parental-Involvement Laws Threaten Young Women's Safety," January 1, 2013. www .prochoiceamerica.org.

NARAL Pro-Choice America   "Refusal Laws: Dangerous for Women's Health," January 1, 2014. www.prochoiceamerica.org.

National Abortion Federation   "Post-Abortion Syndrome," 2010. www.prochoice.org.

National Conference of State Legislatures   "Pharmacist Conscience Clauses: Laws and Information," May 2012. www.ncsl.org.

National Organization for Women   "War on Women's Reproductive Rights Escalates in the States in 2013," January 2014. http://now.org.

Judy Nicastro   "My Abortion, at 23 Weeks," *New York Times*, June 20, 2013.

Randall
O'Bannon

"Why Do Women Have Abortions?
New Study Provides Some Answers,"
LifeNews.com, October 10, 2013.
www.lifenews.com.

Steve Osunsami

"Abortion Billboards: Strong Words
Spark Debate in Atlanta's Black
Neighborhoods," ABC News,
February 22, 2010. http://
abcnews.go.com.

Kim Painter

"Doctors Say Abortions Do
Sometimes Save Women's Lives," USA
Today, October 22, 2012.

Stephanie Pappas

"Providing Abortions Can Be the
Moral Choice, Doctor Says,"
LiveScience, September 12, 2012.
www.livescience.com.

Jeremy W. Peters

"Parties Seize on Abortion Issues in
Midterm Race," New York Times,
January 20, 2014.

Pew Research
Religion & Public
Life Project

"A History of Key Abortion Rulings
of the U.S. Supreme Court," January
16, 2013. www.pewforum.org.

Planned
Parenthood USA

"Medical and Social Health Benefits
Since Abortion Was Made Legal in
the US," January 2013. www
.plannedparenthood.org.

Mary DeTurris
Poust

"What Children Teach Us About
Abortion," US Conference of
Catholic Bishops, January 23, 2013.
http://usccbmedia.blogspot.com.

Kirsten Powers   "Abortion Rights Community Has Become the NRA of the Left," Daily Beast, May 6, 2013. www .thedailybeast.com.

Louise Radnofsky and Ashby Jones   "Support Grows for *Roe v. Wade*," *Wall Street Journal*, January 22, 2013.

Molly Redden   "Hobby Lobby's Hypocrisy: The Company's Retirement Plan Invests in Contraception Manufacturers," *Mother Jones*, April 1, 2014.

Maya Rhodan   "What We Stand to Lose," *Essence*, April 3, 2014.

Gregory J. Roden   "Unborn Children as Constitutional Persons," *Issues in Law and Medicine*, Spring 2010.

Lydia Saad   "Americans Still Split Along 'Pro-Choice,' 'Pro-Life' Lines," Gallup, May 23, 2011. www.gallup.com.

William Saletan   "Do Most Americans Think Most Abortions Should Be Illegal?," *Slate*, January 22, 2014. www.slate.com.

Wesley J. Smith   "Should Doctors Be Forced to Kill?," *Daily Caller*, December 16, 2011.

Akiba Solomon   "The Missionary Movement to 'Save' Black Babies," *Colorlines*, May 2, 2013. http://colorlines.com.

Meredith Somers   "March for Life Expands to New Cause: Obamacare," *Washington Times*, January 20, 2014.

Paul Stark

"Is Abortion Justified When the Unborn Baby Is Disabled?," LifeNews.com, September 25, 2013. www.lifenews.com.

Emily Swanson

"Abortion Poll: Vast Majority Support Legal Abortion for Rape Victims," *Huffington Post*, October 31, 2012. www.huffingtonpost.com.

Sarah Torre

"Conscience Rights: The New Frontline in the Culture War," Heritage Foundation, April 19, 2011. http://blog.heritage.org.

Rick Ungar

"Hobby Lobby Invested in Numerous Abortion and Contraception Products While Claiming Religious Objection," *Forbes*, April 1, 2014.

University of California, San Francisco

"Turnaway Study," Advancing New Standards in Reproductive Health, 2014. www.ansirh.org.

Eddie Velosa

"'Raped' by the Law: Pregnant Victims Fight for Their Rights," RYOT News, September 10, 2013. www.ryot.org.

Cheryl Wetzstein

"Study IDs Reasons for Late-Term Abortions—Age of Women, Financial Issues Factor In," *Washington Times*, December 10, 2013.

Anna Wolfe

"'Personhood' May Be Back," *Jackson Free Press*, March 19, 2014.

Grace Wyler

"Battles over Abortion Flare in 2014," *Time*, February 6, 2014.

Index

A